A Year *with* Father Rutler

FR. GEORGE W. RUTLER

A YEAR

with

FATHER RUTLER

Michaelmas and
Autumn

VOLUME 4

EDITED BY DUNCAN MAXWELL ANDERSON

SOPHIA INSTITUTE PRESS
Manchester, New Hampshire

This book is a selection of Father George Rutler's columns from his weekly parish bulletins dated 2001 to 2017.

Printed in the United States of America. All rights reserved.

Cover and interior design by Perceptions Design Studio.

Excerpts from the *Catechism of the Catholic Church*, Second Edition, for use in the United States of America, copyright © 1994 and 1997, United States Catholic Conference — Libreria Editrice Vaticana. Used by permission. All rights reserved.

Quotations from English translations of papal encyclicals are from the Vatican website (w2.vatican.va) © Libreria Editrice Vaticana. All rights reserved. Used with permission.

Sophia Institute Press
Box 5284, Manchester, NH 03108
1-800-888-9344

www.SophiaInstitute.com

Sophia Institute Press® is a registered trademark of Sophia Institute.

2017 edition

Library of Congress Cataloging-in-Publication Data

Names: Rutler, George W. (George William), author.
Title: A year with Father Rutler : a pastor speaks to his people / George
    William Rutler ; edited by Duncan Maxwell Anderson.
Description: Manchester, New Hampshire : Sophia Institute Press, 2017. |
    Includes bibliographical references.
Identifiers: LCCN 2017024886 | ISBN 9781622823840 (leatherbound : alk. paper)
Subjects: LCSH: Church year meditations. | History, Modern — 21st
    century — Miscellanea.
Classification: LCC BX2170.C55 R884 2017 | DDC 242/.3 — dc23 LC record available at https://lccn.loc.gov/2017024886

2019 edition

978-1-64413-266-1 (vol. 1)
978-1-64413-269-2 (vol. 2)
978-1-64413-272-2 (vol. 3)
978-1-64413-275-3 (vol. 4)
978-1-64413-278-4 (4-volume set)

Library of Congress Control Number:2019954891

First printing

The publication of *A Year with Father Rutler* was made possible through the generosity of:

Sean Fieler
Joseph J. Frank
William Grace
Mr. and Mrs. Vincenzo La Ruffa
Mr. And Mrs. Arthur S. Long

Contents

Michaelmas

The Holy Rosary

All Saints and All Souls

Christ the King

MICHAELMAS

—✳—

ANGELS, SAINTS, AND
OUR MEETING WITH GOD

THAT CHILDREN LEARN THE TRUTH

The beginning of the academic year of many schools in the English-speaking world is called Michaelmas Term. In the British Isles, the traditional feast of St. Michael the Archangel on September 29 marks the end of summer harvest and the beginning of autumn. The opening day of the term has changed little since Shakespeare's time, with

> The whining school-boy with his satchel
> And shining morning face, creeping like snail
> Unwillingly to school.[1]

In 1825, Sir William Curtis (MP) coined the phrase "reading, writing, and arithmetic," which harkens back to the classical Greek and Latin curricula of the trivium (grammar, rhetoric, and logic) and the quadrivium (arithmetic, geometry, music, and astronomy). Pope Sylvester II, who died in 1003, had his own three Rs, having been bishop sequentially of Reims, Ravenna, and Rome. He was one of the most learned popes ever, as well as being the first French one. He invented the pendulum clock and the hydraulic organ, wrote on mathematics, natural science, music, theology and philosophy, and introduced to Europe the decimal system of Arabic numerals. Superstitious folk of the time (including those who resented his restrictions against simony and clerical marriage) read into his three Rs some sign that he had sold his soul to the Devil to get his phenomenal IQ.

---

[1] *As You Like It* II:vii, 7–9.

The liberal arts, as the classical curriculum is known, are called that because they are meant to liberate man from ignorance and indecent slavery to falsehood. This is why tyrants and schemers hate classical learning. In Nazi Germany, Archbishop Josef Frings of Cologne lamented: "The clergy are no longer allowed to give instruction in the elementary schools, and religious instruction has been reduced to a minimum, if not cut altogether." This was not a threat exclusive to Germany or occupied Belgium or Vichy France. In neutral Ireland the bishops opposed a "School Attendance Bill," eventually ruled unconstitutional by the highest judiciary bench, the *Cúirt Uachtaracha*, which would have required parents to send children only to state-approved schools.

Pope Pius XII called the Catholic schools in the United States our Church's greatest treasure. The encroaching servile state compromises that. Already debilitated by attrition (in fifty years, school enrollment in the Archdiocese of New York has dropped by nearly 150,000), there is a danger that the state will structure the curriculum in ways that contradict the liberating philosophy of classical education, and do so without consulting pastors and parents. A government-sponsored "universal pre-kindergarten" program requires that Catholicism be taught only generically, and that religious objects in our classrooms be concealed. This disdains the fact that frees the mind from servility to the state: the three Rs need the great R of religion.

Archbishop Frings later became a cardinal (and his theological adviser would become Pope Benedict XVI). He told the civil government, in words broadcast over the Vatican Radio:

> It is the parents' duty to see that the children learn the truth, the more so since everything is done on the other side to imbue our children with an un-Christian spirit and to prejudice them against the Church of Christ.

October 5, 2014

WONDERS BEYOND OUR REASON

The feast of the Archangels, Michael, Gabriel, and Raphael, on September 29, is quickly followed by the feast of the Guardian Angels on October 2. Here we get into a deep science: not the natural science that increasingly is opening up the wonders of the physical universe, but rather the higher science of perfect spirits and incalculable intelligences, whose lowest "choirs" are the angels and archangels. Unlike natural science, this knowledge comes not from observation but from revelation. We use reason to acknowledge that there are wonders beyond our ability to reason, and that includes angels, who have no need of reason because they are pure intellects.

Angels are creatures, but they existed before the first man (Col. 1:15–16). They are subject to Christ (1 Pet. 3:21–22). They enjoy the constant presence of God (Luke 1:19). They are numerous beyond human calculation, and so they are described as thousands upon thousands, or myriads, since Hebrew has no word for "millions" (Heb. 12:22–23). They know God's will but do not know all its details (Matt. 24:36). Angels are multilingual (1 Cor. 13:17) and patrol the earth (Zech. 1:10–11). Although Christ is divine, He can appear as an angel (Hos. 12:4–5). Angels can appear as winds and fire (Heb. 1:7) and they rejoice when we go to confession (Luke 15:7). Scripture never says that they have halos, and only seraphim and cherubim are described as having wings, so we would probably not recognize an angel if we saw one. They are astonishingly strong, so that one was able to slay 185,000 Assyrians. They want to comfort us (Matthew 28:1–7) and do not want us to give them the worship that is due to God alone (Col. 2:18–19). Jesus had power to invoke

72,000 of them (twelve legions) had He wanted to avoid crucifixion, but He did not (Matt. 26:52–53). At the end of the created universe they will accompany Jesus in the Final Judgment (Matt. 25:31).

As angels have no bodies, they have no size, and so they care for everyone equally, regardless of size or age or worldly importance. Jesus said that the littlest human body has a guardian angel in heaven (Matt. 18:10). In each of us the guardian angels see their Lord and Our Lord. So Pope Francis said on September 20: "Every child that isn't born, but is unjustly condemned to be aborted, has the face of Jesus Christ."[2]

St. Pius of Pietrelcina (Padre Pio) wrote to a young girl: "Never say you are alone in sustaining the battle against your enemies. Never say you have nobody to whom you can open up and confide. You would do this heavenly messenger a grave wrong."

September 29, 2013

---

[2] Pope Francis, address to participants in the meeting organized by the international federation of Catholic medical associations, September 20, 2013.

The Godless, Who Demand Worship

Without question, the Church in China will become the most dynamic force in the Christian world when it emerges from its current persecution. To begin with, the world will be astonished at its size, far surpassing reported numbers. While the Holy See is trying to work out some sort of accord with the Chinese government, which has attempted to impose a state-controlled substitute Church — something of a repetition of the schemes of the Tudor and Gallican schismatics — martyrdoms continue. Recently Bishop Han Dingxiang, an "underground" prelate loyal to the papacy, died in police custody after thirty-one years in prisons and labor camps. The Chinese government said, "We don't know this person and don't know anything about him."

Meanwhile, in the Orwellian state of North Korea, the army has issued a document in response to the spread of Christianity among the troops. Religion is "spreading like a cancer inside North Korea's armed forces, whose mission is to defend Socialism.... It must be eradicated without delay since it comes from our enemies from around the world."[3] In echoes of the Roman emperors, the only worship permitted is the state cult of Kim Jong-Il and the late Kim Il-Sung. In three persecutions in the nineteenth century, at least eight thousand Koreans were martyred. Many of them were canonized in 2000, giving Korea claim to the most saints of any country. More than three hundred thousand have "disappeared"

---

[3] Joseph Yun Li-sun, "Religion Spreading Among Soldiers, Secret Directive Issued to Eradicate It," China Aid Association, September 13, 2007, http://www.chinaaid.org/.

since the end of the Korean War in 1953, and no priest or nun from that period survives. Around one hundred thousand Christians are in labor camps, and accounts of executions are too horrific to describe.

As this situation is inconvenient to the outlook of much of the Western media, it is reported gingerly, if at all. Human rights in religion can be an embarrassment, not least of all to those various professional atheist authors who claim that persecution is something done *by* people of faith and not *to* them. Brutal facts contradict the naïve argument that a godless culture would be a kind and gentle one.

To be a Christian anywhere in our world is to be a sign of contradiction. In our sanctuary are new icons of the Chinese martyr Augustine Zhao Rong, the Korean martyr Andrew Kim Taegon, and Charles Lwanga, the martyr of Africa where the growing Church is also a threatened Church. The news that Pope Benedict XVI may journey to our shores in April of next year "to confirm the brethren" as the successor of St. Peter and Vicar of Christ is a sign that he recognizes how the Church is tested in different ways, some subtler and less lurid than others, wherever she is faithful. This is to be remembered whenever a parish or diocese or nation is distracted by smaller concerns. To be faithful only in fair weather is to be entirely unfaithful.

September 30, 2007

Christ through the Airwaves

I was reminded of the universality of the modern communications revolution the other day when an Australian film producer came to the rectory and showed me a laptop computer he had shown to Sister Lucia, the last surviving visionary of Fatima. It was the first computer she had ever seen, and she enjoyed touching a few of the keys. I touched those keys in the hope that my feeble computer skills might improve.

It does no good to lament the corruption of much of the media, for electronic means of communication are morally indifferent. Like music and atomic energy and any other material reality, they can serve Christ or the Antichrist, and we are accountable for what we do with them. We have seen recently the consequences of the media deliberately distorting what the Pope says. But never before have the Pope and other noble voices been able to reach so many people. It was a great privilege for me as a student in Rome to know the widow of the inventor of the radio. The Marchesa Marconi took delight in showing me pictures of her husband standing by proudly as Pope Pius XI became the first Pontiff to be heard around the world on Vatican Radio. Last Tuesday, Neil Armstrong passed through our parish, and I recalled the thrill of his voice from the moon in 1969.

Eighteen years ago, I began doing programs on the Eternal Word Television Network (EWTN), which has become the largest religious network in the world. During the course of the year, we have many visitors from various continents who have seen our church on the screen in their own countries. Ironically, that network that reaches the globe had a hard time getting access to our own metropolitan New York area. Finally it has, through the efforts of many volunteers, and at the 11:00 a.m. Mass next Sunday, October 8, I shall be able to welcome them as they attend and give thanks for the fruits of their hard work. In a few weeks, our own archdiocese will launch radio broadcasting on the Catholic Channel on SIRIUS Satellite Radio.

Leaders in communications often worship here inconspicuously. Last Monday, a WABC radio host read on air an item from our parish bulletin, which she had seen at Mass the day before. At that same Mass was a former head of National Public Radio. We must not underestimate the potential of the media for good. While some "movers and shakers" in the communications field may have an unworthy agenda, many are just misinformed, and others simply lack the mental equipment to interpret the great truths. As Pope John Paul II confronted Marxism, so our Pope is confronting terrorism and, pray God, he will have the same success. I am sure the first Apostles of Rome, Peter and Paul, would have loved the Internet.

October 1, 2006

THOSE WHO WILL NOT SEE

The parable of the Rich Man and Lazarus (Luke 16:19–31) is the only one of the twenty-four parables that mentions a proper name. Our Lord anticipated the raising of his friend Lazarus, which was the efficient cause of Christ's arrest. "If they will not listen to Moses and the prophets, neither will they be persuaded if someone should rise from the dead." More poignantly, Christ is poorer than Lazarus: "Though Our Lord Jesus Christ was rich, he became poor, so that by his poverty you might become rich" (2 Cor. 8:9).

Dickens most likely was moved by this parable when he wrote his *Christmas Carol*, with the ghost of Jacob Marley returning to warn Scrooge about the course of his life. But in the parable, no ghost returns to warn the rich man's brothers, because they would refuse to believe. Such is the obtuseness of the human will: in the face of facts, some people withdraw into a parallel universe, like the rich man insulated behind his safe gates. Emile Zola did that when he denied the miracle he had witnessed at Lourdes. The saints are likewise ignored by our media because they are a threat to the artificial lifestyle adopted by a synthetic culture slipping into the "netherworld."

In 1974, Aleksandr Solzhenitsyn walked through Paris, bearing the scars of his years in the Gulag. He was a sign of contradiction against the intellectuals who were toying with Marxism without having to pay the price it exacted in the real world. One student at the Sorbonne said that in the few weeks Solzhenitsyn was with them, he exposed the superficiality of their existence. But many continued in their self-absorbed world of illusion.

So it was when Pope Benedict went to the United Kingdom. The media described a looming disaster, and the vitriol against the Pope shocked any fair-minded person. Even sympathetic voices said the trip should be canceled, rather the way Peter tried to block the path of Jesus to Jerusalem. The singularly uninformed Roger Cohen of the *New York Times* speculated: "It remains to be seen whether a service Friday in Westminster Abbey, where the coronation of Henry VIII and Catherine was held, can ease tensions. I doubt it."[4]

The tremendous success of the papal trip converted many, and puzzled others, but there remain those who will not be persuaded "if someone should rise from the dead." Like a bad weather forecaster, they will blithely continue with no mention of their hollow predictions. Some said the Pope should be denied "the honor of a state visit."[5] In retrospect, it was the Pope who honored the land he visited, and we can adapt what *Punch* said when Blessed John Henry Newman was created a cardinal: "'Tis the good and great head that would honor the Hat. Not the Hat that would honor the head."

October 3, 2010

---

[4] Roger Cohen, "A Pope in a Schismatic Isle," *New York Times*, September 16, 2010, http://www.nytimes.com/.
[5] Ibid.

St. Francis, Bold Crusader against Islam

On October 4, we give thanks for one of the best known and least known of all saints. Least known, that is, because Francis of Assisi was not a garden gnome or a doe-eyed hippie, skipping with animals and hugging trees. Garden gnomes do not bear the Stigmata of Christ's wounds. A vegetarian? He berated a friar for wanting to abstain from meat on a feast day and threatened that on Christmas he would "smear the wall with meat." An iconoclast? He was meticulous in the ceremonials of the Mass, insisting that every sacred vessel and vestment be the best, and his Rule dismissed any friar who parted from the Pope on the slightest article of faith. A pacifist? He joined the Fifth Crusade, which had been simmering ever since eleven thousand Muslims had invaded Rome and desecrated the tombs of Peter and Paul in 846.

Francis went to North Africa in 1219 to convert the Muslims and confronted Sultan al Malik al-Kamil, who had just slaughtered five thousand Christians at Damietta. Francis fearlessly told the Sultan: "It is just that Christians invade the land you inhabit, for you blaspheme the name of Christ and alienate everyone you can from His worship." While counselors called for the beheading of Francis according to Muslim law, the sultan was so taken with the humility of Francis that he only had him beaten, chained, and imprisoned, and then he released him.

We are engaged in similar challenges today. Of course, we are aware of the crisis in the Middle East, but the strife is worldwide. Consider Nigeria, whose Catholic population in the last century has soared to nearly twenty million. Last week, under Muslim pressure, the government stopped the Eternal Word Television Network from broadcasting. I have worked with this worldwide Catholic network for twenty-five years and have many Nigerian friends. Two days after the Nigerian bishops objected to this censorship, a Catholic church was destroyed by Muslims, who killed or wounded many worshippers. These events seem to have passed under the radar of our own government and mainstream media.

May St. Francis be our model in how to deal with the threats of our day—not enfeebled by sentimentality and relativism, but armed with a Franciscan zeal for the conversion of souls. We may not have St. Francis's charm, but we have in our hearts and churches the same God. By the way, the popular "Prayer of Saint Francis," which begins, "Make me a channel of your peace," was actually the work of an anonymous author who published it in France in 1912. Its vague theology and lack of mention of Christ express a semi-Pelagian heresy unworthy of the saint of Assisi.

Let the last words of the real saint of Assisi be our guide: "I have done what was mine to do; may Christ teach you what you are to do. Do not seek to follow in the footsteps of the men of old; seek what they sought."

September 30, 2012

To Understand Life Itself

In the eight years of my pastorate here, we have had 360 weddings, and many more are on schedule. This gives us an extended parish family, for couples go from here all over the world as well as enriching our local parish, and many of their parents and relatives make a point of visiting when they come to the city. A chief joy is baptizing the children born of these marriages as well as welcoming couples who come from distances to celebrate their anniversaries.

In filling out marriage forms, I have been surprised by the number of young people who, having graduated with distinction from many of our nation's oldest and most famous universities, cannot write. This is literally so, to indulge the pun. In our computer age, cursive writing is taught less. I have a dear friend who at the age of 105 writes beautiful script, but I also have many friends in their early 20s who scribble their names with the equivalent of the X, which was the legal mark of former generations who had not the privilege of schooling. I admit that, at the same time, the average third-grader is likely to be more computer-savvy than I am. But I do think it a pity that the art of putting hand to paper is being lost, as it both preserves the letters, which are the record of culture, and gives time to think before engraving the thought.

Pope Benedict XVI is certainly one of the most literate popes of history and thinks so clearly that he is easy to understand. This makes fuzzy thinkers a bit nervous. Last week, at Charles University in Prague, he graciously said some indicting things about how educators fail to think. He reminded the audience that their university had been established in 1347 by a pope, Clement VI, and that the Church has always insisted that objective truth rather than subjective opinion is the guarantor of academic freedom. Schools that stress technical knowledge over the cultivation of virtue isolate reason from truth. The attitude that "everything is relative" and that there are no constant moral norms for living, turns philosophy into ideology and threatens free thought. "Fidelity to man requires fidelity to the truth, which alone is the guarantee of freedom."[6]

I was struck by the way the Pope summarized the great vision of Cardinal Newman's *Idea of a University*. Facts are not enough. Education must show how various articles of knowledge relate in an organic and unified understanding of life itself.

Schools should not be factories churning out useful information. Man without a soul seeks only what he thinks is "useful." Man who understands that he is in the image of God seeks beauty, truth, and goodness. This is worth pondering as our own local schools begin a new year.

October 4, 2009

[6] Pope Benedict XVI, Encyclical *Caritas in Veritate*, June 29, 2009, no. 9.

THE APPROVAL OF MAN? OR GOD?

Some papal customs are rooted in the Roman imperium, which sought to destroy Christianity violently, only to be defeated by Christians pacifically. As the Caesars wore red slippers symbolic of the blood of their vanquished foes, so popes have been shod in the same red in token of the martyrs who shed their own blood for Christ.

At papal coronations, flax would be burned before the Pontiff by a master of ceremonies saying: *Sancte Pater, sic transit gloria mundi* (Holy Father, thus passes the glory of the world). This parallels the custom of having a slave sit beside a Roman general in his chariot as he rode in triumph through the Forum while thousands cheered, whispering: *Respice post te, hominem te memento* (Look behind, and remember that you are only a man).

From the singular experience that only 266 men in history have shared, popes have known how ephemeral celebrity can be. In 1846, Pope Pius IX was hailed as the paladin of the new progressive age. Garibaldi wrote from Uruguay to offer military assistance, and Roman youths unhitched the pope's horses so that they themselves might pull his carriage through the cheering crowds. By the end of his reign, Pius IX's funeral had to be held under cover of night, and a mob tried to toss his coffin into the Tiber.

When streets happily were lined with people cheering Pope Francis I last week, his paternal emotions may have been mixed with the thought that not all of those taking his picture would be in church on Sunday. Flattery is not fidelity, nor is enthusiasm the substance of faith. In 1914, when the papal tailor told Pope Benedict XV that he knew he would be elected, the somewhat ill-shapen Pope asked: "If you knew, why didn't you make me a cassock that fits?" Popes know that celebrity is diaphanous and cheers last as long as the breeze. A Gallup poll claims that the public approval of Pope Francis dropped from 72 percent to 59 percent in the past year.

St. Paul had benign contempt for that way of measuring an apostle: "For am I now seeking the approval of man, or of God? Or am I trying to please man? If I were still trying to please man, I would not be a servant of Christ" (Gal.1:10).

When St. Peter walked through Rome, he was not a celebrity like those Plutarch wrote about in his *Parallel Lives*, which was the equivalent of a glossy Hollywood magazine. But few today remember Camillus or Coriolanus or Sertorius. One caution about a Pope addressing a Parliament, a Congress, a Bundestag, or the United Nations is that it might give the impression that he is merely a statesman, and when pop stars surround him, the predilection might be to confuse him with them. This is why it is important to remember the blood of the martyrs and the burning flax.

October 4, 2015

THE DEFENSE OF LIFE

This Tuesday we shall remember another October 7, in 1571, when the Battle of Lepanto was fought off the western coast of Greece, the largest naval operation until the Normandy invasion in 1944. The Holy League, put together by Pope St. Pius V, had 212 fighting ships to turn back the Muslim invasion of Europe by 278 war vessels of the Ottoman Turks. Our world, and our little corner of it in New York, would be unrecognizable today had the outcome of that five-hour battle been reversed. St. Pius made that day a feast of the Holy Rosary in thanksgiving for Our Lady's intercessions, and added to her titles "Our Lady of Victories."

We are now engaged in a clash of cultures even more widespread, and to reduce it to a mere political or economic paradigm would be to ignore its spiritual significance. Observers have remarked a parallel with the moral test the Church faced in World War II, when Blessed Clemens August Cardinal von Galen of Münster risked his life to preach against the eugenics policies sanctioned in his country. Today, bishops are also moved to speak out in defense of life when it is threatened in an unprecedented way. October 4–5 is Respect Life Weekend, and Bishop Joseph F. Martino of Scranton has written a pastoral letter recalling the Church's duty to speak prophetically.[7]

---

[7] During the 2008 campaign, the Democratic Party nominees for president and vice president, Barack Hussein Obama and Joseph Biden, respectively, were notable for their long public records in favor of abortion and were endorsed by the political arm of Planned Parenthood. Biden, a Senator from Maryland, claimed to be a practicing Catholic, had been raised in Scranton, and was campaigning heavily in that diocese among

Bishop Martino, whom I knew when we were students in Rome, is a fine historian who did the research for the canonization cause of St. Katherine Drexel. In his letter, he quotes his predecessor, Bishop Timlin: "The taking of innocent human life is so heinous, so horribly evil, and so absolutely opposite to the law of Almighty God that abortion must take precedence over every other issue. I repeat. It is the single most important issue confronting not only Catholics, but the entire electorate." Bishop Martino reminds his people, "It is incumbent upon bishops to correct Catholics who are in error regarding these matters. Furthermore, public officials who are Catholic, and who persist in public support for abortion and other intrinsic evils should not partake in or be admitted to the sacrament of Holy Communion."[8]

A writer for *U.S. News and World Report* has accused the bishop of Scranton of violating the First Amendment by denying Communion to anyone who publicly contradicts the Church. This turns inside out the amendment that forbids the government to interfere with the free practice of religion. Blessed Clemens von Galen well knew such stratagems of the media to intimidate the Church. Pope Benedict XVI, a successor

---

working-class Catholics to help win Pennsylvania's electoral votes for the Democrats. At the same time, Sen. Robert Casey Jr., Democrat of Pennsylvania, unlike his late father, Robert Casey, the pro-life governor of Pennsylvania, unfailingly voted in favor of abortion, yet campaigned in Scranton for himself and other Democrats as a Catholic. The mainstream news media and the left-wing Catholic press were scandalized that Bishop Martino was running his diocese as if faithfulness to his mandate to protect Catholic teaching mattered. In November 2008, the Democrats did win the state and the election. (They lost both in 2016.)

Very few of Bishop Martino's brother bishops have followed his example in enforcing church law against politicians who present themselves to receive Holy Communion after having publicly and unrepentantly promoted abortion. The following year, 2009, Bishop Martino, citing work-related insomnia and exhaustion, resigned his diocese at the early age of sixty-three.

8   Bishop James C. Timlin, D.D., "The Ballot and the Right to Life," *Catholic Light*, September 23, 2000.

of St. Pius V and also a fervent disciple of von Galen, has said: "God is so humble that he uses us to spread his Word."[9] Neither powerful armies nor minor journalists can stop that.

October 5, 2008

---

[9] Benedict XVI, celebration of Vespers with priests, members of religious orders, seminarians, and deacons, Notre Dame Cathedral, Paris, September 12, 2008.

Armed with a Rosary

October is dedicated to the Holy Rosary and Our Lady of Victory because of the Battle of Lepanto. In 1565, 600 Knights of St. John, commanding an army of 8,000, were defending Malta, having been driven from Rhodes by the Ottoman Turks in 1522. The Muslim armies were conquering Arabia, Iraq, Syria, and North Africa and had defeated the Hungarians in 1526. Their plan was to eradicate Christian naval forces from the Mediterranean in order to invade all Europe. When Cyprus was attacked in 1570, Pope Pius V, a Dominican friar and saint, formed an alliance of the Papal States, Spain, Genoa, Venice, and the Knights of Malta. The Pope's Holy League formed a fleet of 300 ships and 30,000 men—roughly the size of the Muslim forces. It was under the command of Don Juan of Austria, who was only in his twenties, and his assisting admirals were Alvaro de Bazan, Andrea Doria, Agostin Barbarigo, and Sebastian Veniero.

Don Juan, the half brother of the King of Spain, was an illegitimate son of the Holy Roman Emperor Charles V by a popular singer of the day named Barbara Blomberg. He was a bold and highly skilled young commander. Using 50,000 rowers and calculating wind speed, Don Juan engaged the Turkish fleet, under the command of Ali Pasha, off the southern coast of Greece in the Gulf of Lepanto. The battle raged for five hours on October 7, 1571. The Holy League's losses were 8,000 men killed. The Turks lost 25,000. Among the rescued were 12,000 Christians whom the Muslims had been using as galley slaves. It was the largest naval operation between that of Actium in 30 B.C. and the D-Day Invasion of 1944.

In Rome, far from Lepanto, and long before television and radio and telephones, St. Pius V was not certain of what day the battle would be fought, but was inspired on October 7 to assemble a group in the Basilica of Santa Maria Maggiore to pray the Rosary for victory. Then he shouted out that God had just given the Catholic army a great victory. He had a vision in which he saw the battle just as it had been fought.

Christians believe in "linear" history, which is a progress of time toward a goal, guided providentially by God for a purpose. Similar to the ancient Greeks, Muslims believe in "cyclical" history, in which time repeats itself in a succession of events, overseen but not guided by God, although there is moral accountability for what one does in time. In both views, dates are important; in the linear order as instructive, in the cyclical order as repetitive. While the Battle of Lepanto ruined the Turkish force of seventy-five thousand, the Ottomans rallied and besieged Vienna in 1683, and finally were defeated by a Christian alliance headed by the Polish king Jan III Sobieski on September 11.

Armed with no fleet, but with a Rosary, Pope Benedict XVI will be in Turkey November 28–30. For the good of souls, and for peace in the world, this is a time for prayer.

October 15, 2006

Peace versus Pacifism

In these critical days[10] I often ask Our Lady of Victory in the intercessory prayers of the Mass to guide and protect our president, our armed forces, and our allies. I served for three years in the Church of Our Lady of Victory downtown, but I invoke her for more than nostalgic reasons. Mary was given a feast day under the title of Our Lady of Victory after Pope St. Pius V was convinced that her miraculous intercession had saved Christian Europe from the Ottoman Turks at the Battle of Lepanto on October 7, 1571.

Some may ask, "Shouldn't we pray for peace instead of victory?" Peace is the desire of every prayer, bearing in mind that without victory in a just war there can be no peace. St. Augustine explained what makes a war just, and St. Thomas reminds us that it would be sinful not to fight for justice.

The Church, which is the world's most cogent means of peace, rejects pacifism. The pacifist denies the justice of any war and the good of self-defense. In the encyclical *Centesimus Annus*, the Holy Father recalls how much suffering was caused by the political compromises of the

---

[10] This column was written as the U.S. military was in the final preparations for an attack on Afghanistan — to remove the Taliban government harboring Osama bin Laden, the Saudi terrorist who plotted and financed the attack on the World Trade Center less than a month earlier on September 11. As it happened, the U.S. and British bombers began their strikes on Kabul a few hours after this column reached parishioners — on Sunday, October 7, 2001, which was 429 years to the day after the Battle of Lepanto.

Yalta Conference. Every strategy must try to avoid violence to innocent civilians, who are the most tragic victims of wars. Justice seeks only to vindicate the just and punish the guilty. Clumsy minds do not distinguish between retribution and revenge, between victory and vengeance.

The Christian knows that just wars are not exercises in vengeance. They are regrettable but necessary occasions to prove that "Greater love has no man than that he lay down his life for his friends" (John 15:13).

Instruction on Applause in Church[11]

If the need arises, parishioners may politely explain to our non-Catholic friends, whom we warmly welcome, that Catholic custom is against applause in church. Since worship is not entertainment, it is inappropriate to applaud anyone involved in the liturgy, be they priests, or honored guests, or musicians. This is more than a question of good taste. It is a matter of theology.

Mass should be followed by silence conducive to private prayer. Bad habits have been seeping into many Catholic churches. The ordination liturgy permits a ritual acclamation. The one other traditional exception is for the Sovereign Pontiff, who is the Vicar of Christ. Until some happy day when a Pope visits our church, let us avoid applause and offer praise only to God.

October 7, 2001

---

[11] The statement on applause in church was one of Father Rutler's first measures to reestablish Catholic protocol in the parish in the presence of the Blessed Sacrament—practices fallen into disuse in many places.

LIVING PRAYER

Feasts are reminders that we are invited to the eternal Feast in Heaven. As we have noted, October 7 is the feast of the Holy Rosary, instituted to celebrate the victory of Pope St. Pius V's alliance of naval forces against the Islamic Ottomans. Even some English Protestants joined the effort in realization that everything Christianity had given us was at stake. The Pope attributed the victory of the sea battle at Lepanto to the prayers of the Rosary. Among the fruits of that victory must be counted respect for human life, universities, plastic and musical arts, the sacredness of marriage, the equality of women, and the use of reason.

These gifts of Christian culture are vanishing today by default of nominal Christians who have abandoned the Faith that shaped their culture. Our cultural struggle is wider and longer than Lepanto. Young men preparing for the priesthood now are enlisting in history's greatest spiritual struggle. Happily, more men are now enrolled in seminaries in the United States than in nearly two decades: a 16 percent increase since 1995 and 10 percent more than in 2005. As priests, they will support the faithful laity as the faithful support them.

Attacks on Christianity are drawn in blood in places such as Pakistan, Syria, and Nigeria. We may be blindsided if we think the dangers are any less in our own country. The enemy uses cynicism and social pressure rather than weapons of steel.

The prayers of Our Lady are our great defense. Pope Francis's formal announcement in sonorous Latin that Popes John XXIII and John Paul II will be canonized next April affirms their desire that we enlist the Rosary in the crusade against Satan and all his evil works. In 1961 John

XXIII signed the Apostolic Letter *Il Religioso Convegno*, along with his personal meditations on the mysteries of the Rosary, which he perpetually recited in between the duties of his daily schedule. In 2002, John Paul II signed the Apostolic Letter on the Rosary, *Rosarium Virginis Mariae*, as his "favorite prayer" and gave us the Luminous Mysteries to guide us in the darkness of these new days.

Our Lord warned against the "vain repetition" of the Pharisees, who thought that the number of prayers apart from the devotion of the will could bend the ear of God. But vain repetition does not invalidate repetition altogether: the repetitious breathing of the lungs and beating of the heart give physical life; so too does the repeating of the words of Gabriel and of Elizabeth and of Our Lord's own prayer open the gates of eternity. We often bury our beloved dead with rosaries. My own mother had in her hands a rosary that John Paul II had given her. But we who are alive must make the Rosary a living prayer, and by so praying we may live forever.

October 6, 2013

BORN YESTERDAY

Monsignor Ronald Knox, probably the most inspired preacher and apologist of the twentieth century, wrote an essay satirizing some skeptical biblical literary critics, in which he used their methods to "prove" that the real author of Tennyson's "In Memoriam" was Queen Victoria.

Many who doubt the plausibility of the Scriptures are gullible about hoaxes. I don't just mean the rabbit with antelope horns called a "jackalope." There was also the Cardiff Giant of 1869 promoted by P. T. Barnum, and John Payne Collier's forgery of Shakespeare's letters. Some pretended to be the Grand Duchess Anastasia, and far earlier was the hoax of a lady pontiff named Pope Joan. The New York Zoo hoax of 1874 convinced many that animals had escaped. In 1912 there was the Piltdown Man. Henry Ford promoted the "Protocols of the Elders of Zion." There were the aliens landing in Roswell, New Mexico, in 1947, and the Balloon Boy hoax in 2009. The Da Vinci Code claimed an albino monk hid corpses nearby on Thirty-Fourth Street. I confess that I keep a warm spot in my heart for the Loch Ness Monster, which also intrigued Pope Pius XII — who discussed it with the above-mentioned Monsignor Ronald Knox. Unfortunately, Nessie's primary witness was an English vicar, and such testimony is not potent in courts of law.

Hoaxes gain credibility when they use respected sources. In 1938, Orson Welles's adaptation of H. G. Wells' *War of the Worlds* convinced thousands because it was broadcast on radio. Monsignor Knox did something similar on the BBC. People today are inclined to believe hoaxes because they are mentioned witlessly in the mainstream media.

Five years ago, the *New York Times* spent a lot of printer's ink on a bogus ossuary claimed to be that of a "brother" of Christ. Recently, the same journal announced on its front page the discovery of a parchment claiming that there was a Mrs. Jesus. Shortly thereafter, the parchment was adjudged a forgery. If a correction ever appears, I suspect it will be in fine print, back near the Shipping News.

Since journalists often invoke pretentious scholarship to question the authenticity of the Shroud of Turin and the Tilma of Guadalupe, the question begged is, "Why do these people suddenly become naïve and credulous toward improbable claims that contradict Christian inspiration?" The question answers itself. The *New York Times* would be delighted to find that Christ did not radically contradict the norms of His age by forsaking all else and calling others to do the same as a proclamation of the Mystical Union between Christ as Bridegroom and the Church as Bride.

The media should take the counsel of St. Paul, who probably would be fired after his first day at work as an editor of the *New York Times:* "I say again what we have said before: If anyone preaches any gospel other than that which ye received, let him be anathema" (Gal. 1:9).

October 7, 2012

THE FIRST AMENDMENT DOES NOT
MANDATE AN ATHEIST GOVERNMENT

On October 1, former U.S. Attorney General William Barr gave a stirring address to the First Friday meeting of the Guild of Catholic Lawyers in our undercroft. In vivid terms, he analyzed the cultural war that now engages us and the problems caused by the judiciary's usurpation of the legislating function of government. As cultures are shaped by the reception or rejection of eternal truths, our present cultural war is a spiritual one. At stake are the basic facts of natural law, the right to life, the institutions of marriage and the family, and objective moral order as a reference for social liberties and constraints.

The most important issue in the forthcoming national elections is so volatile that it is largely unspoken: the appointment of justices to the Supreme Court. That will determine the fate of our spiritual combat. Whenever these subjects are raised, those who deny the objectivity of truth invoke the "wall of separation" between Church and state as a smokescreen for the diminution of moral perceptions. There is a palpable hypocrisy in those who cite this disestablishment principle to intimidate Catholics and Evangelicals—while themselves using the pulpits of sympathetic sects to advance their political campaigns. Social engineers who want to legalize abortion, assisted suicide, infanticide, and other moral offenses must criminalize God.

The dissenting opinion of Chief Justice William Rehnquist in *Wallace v. Jaffree* eloquently explains how prejudiced parties misuse the concepts of "separation of church and state" and the "wall of separation" between them. The First Amendment to the U.S. Constitution prohibits the establishment of a state church and the favoring of one religion over another. It does not prohibit the free exercise of religion. Thomas Jefferson had nothing to do with that amendment, being in France at that time. But even Jefferson—a Deist, and atypical among our nation's founders for his skepticism—in his second inaugural address as president acknowledged the states' authority to promote religion.

On the day the First Amendment was passed, Washington invoked "prayer" and "Almighty God" in proclaiming a national day of thanksgiving. None of the Founding Fathers would have countenanced the recent abuse of the First Amendment to ban the Ten Commandments from civil discourse or to prohibit state-supported celebrations of Christmas and Easter. The national elections in November will test our religious integrity. Baptism disenfranchises no one. The baptismal renunciations of Satan and all his evil works and all his empty promises are the surest safeguard of our civic integrity.

October 10, 2004

MAKING DISCIPLES

The opening of the Number 7 subway stop down the street is another reminder of the increasing importance of our part of Manhattan. Within the next couple of years, the section called Hudson Yards will have nearly 65,000 more residents. I am frequently asked of this area, "How many of them are Catholic?" Jesus did not send His disciples into Catholic neighborhoods, because there were none. He said, "Go into all the world and proclaim the gospel to all creation" (Mark 16:15). Certainly He envisioned Hudson Yards in that calculus. The proper question about the new people living and working here should be, "How many of them *will* be Catholic?" The answer in large part depends on you and me.

Right now in the Hudson Yards area there are 12,416 households, of which 8,924 are not families. There are 11,243 households without children, and only 1,174 with children. The urban economy explains much of this. New York, next to Washington, DC, is the most expensive city in the nation for rearing children. (My mother always insisted that children are reared, and not raised like vegetables.) Our nation has failed in providing a reasonable economic culture friendly to families with children. The average household net worth in Hudson Yards is $1,048,000, which sounds like a lot, until you factor in the price of real estate and cost of living, not to mention taxes and school costs.

The family is in crisis worldwide, for various reasons, and so it is being addressed by the synod taking place in Rome. "Crisis" is a Greek word that means a moment of testing, but it also means an opportunity. For the Christian, the opportunity is to remind a world that is confused about marriage and procreation—which often tries through civil legislation and judicial imperialism to burlesque nature and nature's God—that Christ has sanctified marriage as a bond between a man and a woman as an indissoluble sign of His unfailing love; and that, through its fecundity in child-bearing, it is a sign of the fruitfulness of love. The bond of marriage is a heavy chain only in the mind of the cynic. For those who love the Lord, the bond is His embrace.

In his homily at the opening of the synod on October 4, Pope Francis summoned the words of Pope Benedict XVI:

> The Church is called to carry out her mission in truth, which is not changed by passing fads or popular opinions. The truth which protects individuals and humanity as a whole from the temptation of self-centeredness and from turning fruitful love into sterile selfishness, faithful union into temporary bonds. "Without truth, charity degenerates into sentimentality. Love becomes an empty shell, to be filled in an arbitrary way. In a culture without truth, this is the fatal risk facing love."[12]

October 11, 2015

---

[12] Benedict XVI, Encyclical *Caritas in Veritate*, June 29, 2009, no. 3.

Our World Parish and
Its Holy Suffering

The Holy Eucharist unites each congregation with our fellow believers throughout the world, along with the faithful departed in Purgatory and the saints in Heaven. Thus, it is often said that the Catholic Church is too universal to be merely "international." The concerns of local churches in other lands should move us from preoccupation with local matters. The word "parochial" is a good one, referring to the parish as the local family of the Church, but "parochialism" can mean an isolated mentality.

The mainstream media have been poor in covering attacks on the Church—for instance, in Vietnam, where the government has been confiscating Church property and intimidating the faithful. The archbishop of Hanoi, Joseph Ngo Quang Kiet, is under virtual house arrest, and Prime Minister Nguyen Tan Dung has threatened "extreme actions" against Catholic protesters.

The situation has been even more volatile in the last month in India, where small but potent groups of Hindu extremists concentrated in Kandhamal have burned down about 4,500 Christian houses, 100 churches, and 20 other church institutions, including convents and rectories. An estimated 50,000 Christians have fled into forests or live now in refugee camps or with relatives and friends in outlying areas. The situation is producing martyrs, such as Lalji Nayak in Orissa, who refused to renounce the Faith at the point of a knife and died of his injuries a few days later. So far, about 50 have been killed, including a nun who was violated and a father and son who were hacked to death. Institutions founded by Mother Teresa and run by her Missionaries of Charity were set on fire, and some of the lepers in their care were blinded by chemicals. The missionaries intend to return as soon as possible to care for patients with leprosy and tuberculosis.

Coincident with this, the first female saint of India will be canonized by Pope Benedict XVI this Sunday, October 12. St. Alphonsa, daughter of Ouseph and Mariam Muttathupandathu, was born in Kottayam in Kerlala and died in 1946 at the age of thirty-six after many illnesses. India's first saint was Gonsalo Garcia, canonized in 1862. Garcia, who was from Vasai, was born of an Indian mother and a Portuguese father in 1556 and was crucified in 1597 in Nagasaki, Japan. It is hoped that soon, Blessed Teresa of Calcutta will also be raised to the altars. Mother Teresa walked through the streets of our parish more than once, and frequently remarked that the difficulties in her own land were not as bad as the materialism and indifference that afflicts so much of our own society. When we pray for our fellow Christians, we are doing a most concrete and practical thing. And when we contribute money, we remember thankfully that part of it regularly goes to help others whose tragic conditions also occasion triumphs of holy religion.

October 12, 2008

IN CONVERSATION WITH OUR MOTHER

Having had father, uncles, and cousins in combat on the high seas for our country, I may have been a disappointment to the family line, being prone to seasickness when doing anything more adventurous than rowing in college. I was taken aboard a Liberty ship in World War II as an infant, but only long enough to be shown to my father and have my diaper changed. So I lay claim to having been on a ship in wartime, although my service was an inferior one.

Naval historians still contend over which was the largest maritime engagement: Salamis in 480 B.C., Jutland in 1916, the Philippine Sea or Leyte Gulf in 1944, but Lepanto in October of 1571 ranks with them in historical importance. As it saved Christian civilization for a while, the Battle of Lepanto may have been the most decisive. Pope St. Pius V organized the battle, and his most critical weapon was the Holy Rosary, which is why the month of October is dedicated to this form of prayer—the most celestial, save the Eucharist itself.

While pious belief attributes the invention of the Rosary to Saint Dominic in his struggle against the Albigensian heretics, who denied the true divine and human natures of Christ, it goes back earlier, to when those monastic lay brothers known as *conversi*, not being able to read, used it as a substitute for the regular recitation of all 150 psalms. Originally, the Rosary consisted of just the Our Father (which is why the lane in London where rosaries were made is still called Paternoster Row). During the twelfth century, the first half of the Hail Mary was added, and the second half was added somewhat later. Gradually, meditation on various mysteries was encouraged. St. John Paul II enriched the Rosary with the Luminous Mysteries. It is called a Rosary because it is a *rosarium*, or "rose garden," and it offers God prayer made fragrant with the words of St. Elizabeth, the Archangel Gabriel, and Christ Himself.

Our civilization now is threatened not only by the heretical forces that engaged the Christians at Lepanto, but also by the subtler forces of atheism, euphemistically called "secularism," that have insinuated themselves into our civil institutions.

In 1985, a priest was deeply moved to see St. John Paul II praying the Rosary humbly on his knees. He said, "I became aware of the density of the words of the Mother of Guadalupe to St. Juan Diego: 'Don't be afraid, am I not perhaps your mother?'" From that moment the priest has never failed to recite all fifteen decades of the Rosary each day, even now that he is Pope Francis.

October 12, 2014

The Future of Religion in America

Roughly 50.2 percent of our nation's population of 281.4 million have some religious affiliation. Catholics are the largest single group at 62 million, while the total of the numerous Protestant denominations is 66 million. In the last ten years, Catholics have experienced an increase of 16.2 percent. This rate is exceeded by only a few small sects.

While the 66 million Protestants have 222,000 congregations, the 62 million Catholics have just 22,000 congregations. Jews, numbering 6 million, have 3,727 congregations, while the 4 million Mormons have 12,000 congregations. Clearly, the Catholic parishes are far larger, and thus those who staff them have far greater responsibilities.

Catholics are the religious majority in 37 states and the District of Columbia. Muslims number 1.6 million, which is less than thought, although methods of counting adherents make it difficult to reach an accurate figure.

The Catholic population declined 14 percent in Rhode Island, the state with the most Catholics per capita, while it increased 45 percent in Arizona and a remarkable 111 percent in Nevada. There were static or declining Catholic numbers in the Midwest and the Northeast, with most growth elsewhere. If present trends continue, by the end of this century, mainstream Protestant denominations, including Presbyterians, Lutherans, and Episcopalians—with respective declines of 9, 5, and 2 percent—will no longer exist as significant entities.

In New York City in the past ten years: Catholics increased from 3,492,670 to 3,617,061; Jews decreased from 1,314,000 to 1,233,900; Muslims had no statistics then and now number 176,814; Baptists decreased from 130,482 to 121,436; Episcopalians decreased from 87,692 to 80,964.

The greatest increases have been among religious groups that are traditional in practice, and the greatest decreases have been among the liberal denominations. This would seem to contradict pundits who urge the Church to water down doctrine to be more "relevant."

The Holy See recently reminded us, in the document *Dominus Iesus*, that only the Catholic Church herself, and the separated Orthodox bodies, can legitimately be recognized as churches. Christian sects or denominations are "ecclesial entities" for whose reconciliation the Church prays. Our children and grandchildren will grow up in a society without the old "mainline" Protestant groups. Two non-Christian groups, the Muslims and Mormons, will take the place of all Protestant denominations excepting the more vigorous Evangelical churches.

Most important, almost half of all Americans have no religious affiliation. Catholics must: (1) renew their own practice of the Faith; (2) in charity summon to unity the non-Christians and lapsed Christians of the disappearing denominations; and (3) convert the 50 percent of our nation who seek God but have not found Him.

October 13, 2002

Single-Mindedness

There was a time—and perhaps with improvements in our schools that time will come again—when schoolboys memorized, among other famous classical lines, the expression: *Ceterum censeo Carthaginem esse delendam.* It was the exasperated call, in the second-century B.C. Senate of the Roman Republic, for the conquest of Carthage in what is now Tunisia. "Furthermore, I say that Carthage must be destroyed." The senator Cato the Elder ended each of his speeches that way, so that it became an inside joke, and his fellow senators chanted it along with him as a kind of ritual.

Churchill said that a fanatic "is one who can't change his mind and won't change the subject." In David Copperfield, the gently simple-minded Mr. Dick was obsessed with writing about the head of King Charles, and "King Charles's Head" has since become a cipher for all sorts of monomania. But Cato was not a futile fanatic, and his obsession was vindicated, albeit some three years after his death, when Carthage, the heart of the North African empire, was indeed destroyed, in flames for days.

Various studies of keys to success in assorted enterprises agree that constant devotion to one goal is crucial. Thomas Edison experimented repeatedly to find the right material for an incandescent light bulb and finally discovered the properties of a carbon filament only after trying hundreds of other materials, including human hair. Was he obsessive? He called it "stick-to-it-iveness" and said that genius is 1 percent inspiration and 99 percent perspiration. "Keep your eyes on the prize," in the words of a folk song. On a loftier plane, the Savior said: "Seek first the Kingdom of God and his righteousness, and all these things shall be added to you" (Matt. 6:33).

There are those who would stifle the pro-life cause by calling it a single-issue obsession. Few would say that about the abolition movement or the struggle against child labor, even though such worthy causes did attract a fair share of distempered monomaniacs. But slaves and children have to be born first, and so the protection of life from conception must rank first among all dedications of philanthropy.

Blessed John Paul II once submitted to an interview with the respected journalist Vittorio Messori, who asked him if he was perhaps "obsessive" in his preaching against abortion. The Holy Father replied: "The legalization of the termination of pregnancy is none other than the authorization given to an adult, with the approval of an established law, to take the lives of children yet unborn and thus incapable of defending themselves. It is difficult to imagine a more unjust situation, and it is very difficult to speak of obsession in a matter such as this, where we are dealing with a fundamental imperative of every good conscience — the defense of the right to life of an innocent and defenseless human being."

October 13, 2013

CRITERIA FOR A JUST WAR

As one long fascinated with historical coincidences, I was particularly struck by the fact that the war against terrorists in Afghanistan was launched by the United States and Britain on October 7, the feast of Our Lady of the Rosary and the anniversary of the Battle of Lepanto in 1571. The war began at the end of our 11:00 a.m. liturgy, during which I preached on the victory of the papal fleet over the Ottoman fleet of Ali Pasha. History is not an exercise in obscurity. The defeat of the Ottoman forces in the sixteenth century has many parallels to our present situation.

Never changing are the criteria for a just war—*jus ad bellum*, as described by St. Augustine more than sixteen hundred years ago:

1. The cause must be just.

2. It must be directed by the legitimate government authority.

3. There must be a noble intent.

4. All other solutions for resolving the dispute must have been exhausted.

5. The resulting good must be greater than resulting damage.

6. There must be a reasonable chance of victory.

7. The ultimate goal must be the establishment of peace.

Once a war begins, it is to be conducted according to two just precepts (*jus in bello*), namely:

1. The force used must not exceed what is required to achieve a just end.

2. Every effort must be made strategically to prevent harm to innocent parties.

In 1982, Pope John Paul II reminded us, "People have the right and even the duty to defend their existence and freedom using proportionate means when they are threatened by an unjust aggressor."[13] Long before, St. Paul told St. Timothy: "God did not give us a spirit of cowardice but rather of power and love and self-control" (2 Tim. 1:7). In any war, and above all in the unending spiritual combat that engages our souls all our lives, what power we have is to be guided by love, and love requires the use of self-control. We may thank God that the Catholic Church, above all human institutions, has refined this moral analysis, never confusing bravery with false heroics or love with sentimentality.

A Helpful Instruction: Eucharistic Ministry

To promote the "reform of the reform" of the Liturgy, and to correct widespread misunderstanding of liturgical norms by well-intentioned people, Pope John Paul II on the feast of the Assumption in 1997 issued an Instruction, *Ecclesiae de Mysterio*, on the collaboration of the nonordained faithful in the sacred ministry of priests. It is a beautifully written meditation on the Eucharistic rituals and may be used as a stimulus for prayer and reflection on the deep mystery of the Holy Eucharist.

Among its guidelines, it reminds us that the ordained clergy are the normative distributors of Holy Communion. In special and infrequent circumstances (*ex temporanea deputatione*), the lay faithful may be called on to assist in the distribution of the Blessed Sacrament, but not on a regular basis (see article 8). Thus, they are properly referred to as "extraordinary

---

[13] St. John Paul II, message for the Day of Peace, January 1, 1982.

ministers" and not "eucharistic ministers." They may also assist the clergy in taking Communion to the sick if there are a large number in need. To get this wrong is to make the mistake of what the Holy Father has described as clericalizing the laity and laicizing the clergy. Such confusion has not helped to encourage priestly vocations.

We want our parish to be a model of the Roman guidelines, setting forth a right image of the economy of worship. Since these are the Holy See's counsels, they are not matters for debate but rather should be received as opportunities to reflect more deeply and joyfully on the way each of us may be of more fruitful service to Christ according to our unique states of life.

(Note: *Ecclesiae de Mysterio* and other documents of the Holy See are available through the bookshop of the Daughters of St. Paul at 115 East Twenty-Ninth Street, between Park and Lexington Avenues.)

October 14, 2001

Spiritual Brilliance

When suave politeness, tempering bigot zeal, corrected 'I believe' to 'one does feel.'" So spoke Monsignor Ronald Knox (1888–1957) even before he converted to Catholicism from Anglicanism. His satire was directed at those who would water down doctrine to mere opinion. That confused kind of thinking, often masked as "broadmindedness" or "liberalism," was what Blessed John Henry Newman said he had spent his life contending against. The two of them logically led up to Pope Benedict XVI, who has called such misunderstanding and abuse of truth the "dictatorship of relativism."

When people inquire about good spiritual reading, I eagerly recommend anything by Knox, especially his collected sermons and retreat addresses, which are easily available. He is unique in his style, which is both easily understood and deceptively profound, woven with shining wit. As a young man, he was heralded as the wittiest man in England. From the depths of his Christian consciousness, he said, "Only man has dignity; only man, therefore, can be funny."

Most of Knox's writing was pastoral: some for students at Oxford, where he was Catholic chaplain; some preached in parishes or on ceremonial occasions; and some given as talks to schoolgirls during World War II. He was a genius as a classical scholar and translated the entire New Testament. He may well have been the finest preacher of the twentieth century. A piece of writing by him almost always has some original insight, and artlessly reveals him as a supreme artist of English letters. He was popular on radio and incidentally wrote entertaining literary criticism and detective novels. There is an admiring biography of him by Evelyn Waugh—who lacked a natural instinct for seeing the best in people. A book about Knox and his remarkable brothers, gifted in their own spheres, was written in 1977 by his niece Penelope Fitzgerald.

While more reserved than G. K. Chesterton, he and Chesterton were close friends, and what Knox preached in Westminster Cathedral after the death of his hero in 1936 describes himself, too: "He had the artist's eye which could suddenly see in some quite familiar object a new value; he had the poet's intuition which could suddenly detect, in the tritest of phrases, a wealth of new meaning and of possibilities. The most salient quality, I think, of his writing is this gift of illuminating the ordinary, of finding in something trivial a type of the eternal."

One reason I mention Knox is that he represents the vast wealth of spiritual brilliance that has been neglected in the last generation. The light of those like Knox should not be hid under a bushel, but placed on a lampstand, where it can give light to the whole house, and that means every parish church, which is God's own house.

October 17, 2010

St. Damien the Leper

Last Sunday, Pope Benedict raised to the altars five new saints: Zygmunt Szczesny Felinski (1822–1895), archbishop of Warsaw; Francisco Coll y Guitart (1812–1875), a Dominican priest; Jozef Damiaan De Veuster (1840–1889), priest of the Congregation of the Sacred Hearts of Jesus and Mary; Rafael Arnáiz Barón (1911–1938), a Trappist religious; and Marie de la Croix (Jeanne) Jugan (1792–1879), who founded the Little Sisters of the Poor.

Jeanne Jugan's homes for the infirm elderly are now in thirty-two countries, and some of their selfless work is in our own archdiocese. A statue of St. Damien represents the state of Hawaii in the United States Capitol. Word of his heroic labors among the lepers on Molokai quickly spread after his death. Theodore Roosevelt instructed the sixteen battleships of the Great White Fleet to dip their flags as they passed Damien's grave. In 1934, Roosevelt's fifth cousin Franklin sent a U.S. naval vessel to transport the body to its native Belgium, where it was received by the king, the cardinal-archbishop, and a hundred thousand people who hailed Father Damien as *De Grootste Belge*—"the Greatest Belgian." One day at Mass, Father Damien spoke to his outcast congregation as "we," for he had contracted the disease himself. Now known as Hansen's disease, leprosy can be treated with drugs first developed in the 1940s. There still are about 2.5 million Hansen's patients in the world. About seventy-five lepers could be cured for the average cost of one cosmetic "face-lift" in New York City.

When Jesus told a young man, perhaps the same age as Damien when he arrived in Hawaii, to get rid of everything that blocked God, "his face fell, and he went away sad, for he had many possessions" (Mark 10:22). Christ the Savior is not a cosmetic surgeon. At the Mass, He does not say, "Lift up your faces," for He bids the people: *Sursum corda* — "Lift up your hearts." St. Damien's face was most beautiful when it became disfigured like the Messiah's: "He is despised and rejected of men; a man of sorrows, and acquainted with grief; and we hid our faces from him" (Isa. 53:3).

Among Father Damien's despisers was a wealthy Presbyterian missionary in Honolulu, the Rev. Dr. Hyde, who, in a letter in 1890 to another missionary, the Rev. H. B. Gage, wrote that the Catholic priest was dirty, headstrong, bigoted, and promiscuous. Robert Louis Stevenson, himself a fair-minded Scots Presbyterian, had visited the leper colony. Upon reading the attack on Father Damien, he published a scorching reply to Dr. Hyde, which included the words: "For if that world at all remember you, on the day when Damien of Molokai shall be named a saint, it will be in virtue of one work: your letter to the Reverend H. B. Gage."

In St. Peter's Square, 119 years later, that prediction was fulfilled.

October 18, 2009

COMIC-BOOK HEROES AND REAL HEROES

L ast week, more than 150,000 people attended the annual New York Comic Con exhibition nearby at the Javits Center. Many had come dressed as their favorite comic-book characters: Batman, Spiderman, Superman, and Wonder Woman. Along with Mickey Mouse, Donald Duck, and Dick Tracy, they added more color to our already interesting neighborhood.

The saints glowing on our windows and the statues reflecting the votive lights testify that Holy Mother Church produces the most fascinating characters, and—unlike the comic-book heroes—these were real. More than that, they changed our world for the better and combatted the real Prince of Lies, who has menaced more people through the ages than any comic-book villain.

In recent days, as eyes look warily and perplexed on the spreading threat of Islam, I have thought of the genuine heroes who confronted that challenge in their various generations. If we are shocked at the genocide of Christians, the beheading of children, the torture and crucifixion of fathers and their young sons, we should remember the real heroes who were familiar with such slaughter in their own day. In Tours in 732, the Frankish king Charles Martel defeated the Islamic army using clever weaponry against great odds. Then there were Richard the Lionheart, St. Louis IX, János Hunyadi, St. John of Capistrano, Don Juan of Austria, Andrea Doria, St. Pius V, and Jan Sobieski, all of whom lived lives that could constitute an entire college course in history, psychology, politics, and religion. If some of these names are now obscure, that is the fault of those who do not appreciate how, if any one of them had failed, our world would be far more miserable today and its institutions unrecognizable, and it is entirely possible that none of us would be alive.

Europe and, to an increasing extent, our own country are experiencing waves of Islamic immigrants who are not welcome in some of their own lands. Mohammed is the most popular name for boys in London now, and Arabic is the fastest-growing language in the United States. Honest and needy refugees expect the Christian welcome that the gospel enjoins, for no one is foreign to Christ. But the spiritual gift of discernment should distinguish the immigrant from the invader, and there is palpable evidence that some people of ill will pretend to be refugees when in fact they are of the ilk that Charles Martel and all those other real heroes confronted.

The popular press downplayed the fact that those men and women in the school in Oregon were killed because they were Christian, albeit by a homegrown fanatic.[14] Perhaps the journalists could not cope with the fact that Christ is being crucified every day in many ways. He predicted that, which is why the figures in our stained-glass windows and beckoning from our statues are not Superman and Wonder Woman, but saints and the Lady who is Queen of Saints.

October 18, 2015

---

[14] On October 1, 2015, a student named Chris Harper Mercer killed eight classmates and the professor in his writing class at Umpqua Community College in Roseburg, Oregon. Surviving shooting victims reported to their families that Mercer told the students to stand up, and then asked whether they were Christians. When they said yes, he replied, "Good, because you're going to see God in about one second" and shot them.

DEFENDER OF THE JEWS

October 9 was the fiftieth anniversary of the death of Pope Pius XII. He lived in one of the most tumultuous papal reigns, and history is still trying to absorb it. Sometimes the books tell more about the historians than the history. Sham scholars twist the annals to fit their theories. So has it become the case with some historians of Pius XII.

As Vatican secretary of state, he had condemned the Nazis before a quarter of a million people at Lourdes. Before that, as nuncio to Germany, he attacked the neo-paganism of National Socialism in almost all of his forty-four public speeches. The Universal Shepherd had the care of millions of persecuted Catholics, including the thousands of clergy imprisoned.

Pius XII sheltered and saved the lives of at least 700,000 Jews, hiding upwards of a tenth of that number right in Rome in 155 religious houses and in the Vatican. This had to be done subtly to avoid retaliation, as happened when the Archbishop of Utrecht in the Netherlands condemned the deportation of Jews, which incited a pogrom in which many were killed, including the convert St. Edith Stein.

Leaders such as Golda Meir thanked the Pope for saving Jewish lives. The Chief Rabbi of Jerusalem wrote: "The people of Israel will never forget what His Holiness and his illustrious delegates, inspired by the eternal principles of religion which form the very foundations of true civilization, are doing for us unfortunate brothers and sisters in the most tragic hour of our history."[15]

---

[15] Chief Rabbi Isaac Herzog (personal note to Pope Pius XII, February 1945).

The Chief Rabbi of Romania said: "The Catholic Church saved more Jewish lives during the war than all other churches, religious institutions and rescue organizations put together. Its record stands in startling contrast to the International Red Cross and the Western democracies." While the U.S. and other allied governments often notoriously rejected refugees, the Vatican forged documents to help thousands of Jews to escape.

The mainstream media in the West largely ignored much of this, and Albert Einstein reflected how the media, along with the universities and law courts in the 1930s, often enabled the horrors: "Only the Church stood squarely across the path of Hitler's campaign for suppressing truth. I never had any special interest in the Church before, but now I feel a great affection and admiration, because the Church alone has had the courage and persistence to stand for intellectual truth and moral freedom."[16]

Today the media, the universities, and the courts once again cooperate with offenses against the most innocent life by advocacy of abortion, euthanasia, genetic experimentation, and general contempt for natural law. At this moment, the American people are being challenged to decide the course of our society, and once again the Catholic Church is a singular and isolated voice for good.

Pius XII's first antecedent said: "Always be ready to give an explanation to anyone who asks you for a reason for your hope, but do it with gentleness and reverence, keeping your conscience clear, so that, when you are maligned, those who defame your good conduct in Christ may themselves be put to shame. For it is better to suffer for doing good, if that be the will of God, than for doing evil" (1 Pet. 3:15–17).

October 19, 2008

---

[16] "Religion: German Martyrs," *Time*, December 23, 1940.

THEIR ENEMY'S ENEMY

While serving as chaplain in a large mental hospital, I quickly learned that one can be both mentally ill and highly intelligent. Hitler, Stalin, Pol Pot, and their superior in malice, Chairman Mao, were intelligent men who vandalized the attics of culture because they had some vestige of culture and hated it.

Thus it is with those who think of themselves as the culturally elect in our day. Politicians and the media that comment on them are the first generation of our society to have been badly schooled without being aware of the fact. Napoleon had the same problem, which is why Talleyrand lamented that a man so highly intelligent had been so poorly educated.

Atheists, who are politely called "secularists," are different from the saints who are "in this world but not of it" because they are "of the world but not in it." This explains why their solutions to the world's ills are so wrong.

Much of the media are reluctant to report, let alone express outrage at, the beheading of Christian infants, the crucifixion of Christian teenagers, the practical genocide of Christian communities almost as old as Pentecost, and the destruction to date of many churches in the Middle East. Why is this moral obliviousness (a sanitized term for what Lenin called "useful idiocy") so instinctive? Very simply, many disdain Judeo-Christian civilization and its exaltation of man in the image of God with the moral demands that accrue to that. Their operative philosophy is that "the enemy of my enemy is my friend."

The Nazis were promoted by many European aristocrats and, until the Nuremburg Racial Laws of 1935, even by some prominent Jewish and other minorities, because the Nazis were seen as a foil to the Bolsheviks and a means to social reconstruction. Conversely, the Stalinists were supported by many Western democrats because they were perceived as the antidote to the Nazis. The U.S. ambassador to the Soviet Union from 1936 to 1938, Joseph Davies, wrote a book, *Mission to Moscow*, that whitewashed Stalin's atrocities. In 1943, with the cooperation of President Roosevelt, Warner Brothers made it into a film that was hailed in the *New York Times* by Bosley Crowther as a splendid achievement. If the Nazis seemed an antidote to the Bolsheviks and vice versa, the bacilli unleashed nearly destroyed the world. Satan is a dangerous vaccine.

There are some today in public positions who underestimate terrorism, in some instances calling it "workplace violence." They are like Ambassador Davies, who said: "Communism holds no serious threat to the United States." Those who see good and evil as abstractions do not expect hatred of the holy to take its toll in reality. The Quran says of Jesus, "They killed him not" (Sura 4). St. Paul says, "For many walk, of whom I have told you often (and now tell you weeping), that they are enemies of the cross of Christ" (Phil. 3:18). To deny the contradiction is to deny reality.

October 19, 2014

"That Scaffold Sways the Future"

It is astonishing how the saints have dealt with challenges and difficulties similar to ours, regardless of differences in their cultures. Consider some whose feasts are this week. St. Juan Capistrano was born in Italy in 1386 and became a prominent lawyer and governor of Perugia when only twenty-six. In his generation, three men claimed to be Pope at the same time; the bubonic plague wiped out one-third of the population, including nearly half of the clergy; the Italian city-states, as well as England and France, were at war with each other; and Islam was threatening Europe. Having become a Franciscan friar, and a very international one before the ease of jet travel, he preached in Italy, Germany, Bohemia, Hungary, Poland, and Russia. Always a man of action, he joined ranks with the Hungarian general John Hunyadi and engaged the Turkish army, against massive odds, at Belgrade in 1456. As the seventy-year-old friar led the charge on horseback, his only weapons were a crucifix and the banner of St. George. His dramatic victory saved our civilization, though he died shortly after from infection.

St. Anthony Claret was a Spaniard of Catalonia in the nineteenth century. The scholar started a huge library at Barcelona to remedy widespread ignorance about the Faith. In the revolutionary period of 1849 he sailed to Cuba, reforming clerical life, establishing a seminary, and regularizing nine thousand marriages. While building a hospital and numerous schools, he inaugurated credit unions for the poor, provided vocational instruction for disadvantaged children, and modernized agricultural methods, working as a farmer in addition to his episcopal duties. Having established the first religious order for women in Cuba, he denounced racial prejudice and improved the prison system. Called back to Spain in 1857, as confessor to Queen Isabella II, he established a museum of natural history, a scientific laboratory, and schools of language and music. In the revolution of 1868 he went with the queen into exile, where he continued missionary work in Paris, dying in France of exhaustion.

Last Sunday, the anniversary of the "miracle of the Sun" in Portugal in 1917, Pope Francis consecrated the world to the Immaculate Heart of Mary before a vast throng in St. Peter's Square. On the same day, 522 martyrs killed by left-wing, anti-Church forces in the 1930s were beatified in Spain. This exceeded even the 492 beatified by Pope Benedict XVI in 2007. Many in our day remain sympathetic toward the martyrs' persecutors and objected to the beatification. While others vaguely allowed that they were "martyrs of the twentieth century," Pope Francis was specific: they were "martyrs killed for their faith during the Spanish Civil War."

While "new occasions teach new duties," in the words of James R. Lowell, saints ancient and modern serve their Lord against the same Foe:

> Yet that scaffold sways the future, and behind the dim
> unknown,
> Standeth God within the shadow, keeping watch above
> His own.

October 20, 2013

LORDS OF THIS WORLD

Exactly eight years ago I wrote a column titled "The One We Were Waiting For," in which I referred to a book by Monsignor Robert Hugh Benson, *The Lord of the World*. That dystopian novel has been cited by Pope Benedict XVI, and Pope Francis said he has read it several times. The protagonist, if one can apply that term to an Antichrist, imposed a new world religion with Man himself as god. His one foe was Christianity, which he thwarted in part by using "compromised Catholics and compliant priests to persuade timid Catholics."

Since then, that program has been realized in our time, to an extent beyond the warnings of the direst pessimists. Our federal government has intimidated religious orders and churches, challenging religious freedom. The institution of the family has been redefined, and sexual identity has been gnosticized to the point of mocking biology. Assisted suicide is spreading, abortions since 1973 have reached a total equal to the population of Italy, and sexually transmitted diseases are at a record high. Objective journalism has died, justice has been corrupted, racial bitterness ruins cities, entertainment is degraded, knowledge of the liberal arts spirals downward, and authentically Catholic universities have all but vanished. A weak and confused foreign policy has encouraged aggressor nations and terrorism while metastasized immigration destroys remnant Western cultures, and genocide is slaughtering Christian populations. The cynical promise of economic prosperity is mocked by the lowest rate of labor participation in forty years, an unprecedented number of people on food stamps and welfare assistance, and the largest disparity in wealth in over a century.

In his own grim days, St. Augustine warned against nostalgia: "The past times that you think were good, are good because they are not yours here and now." The present time, however, might try even his confidence. Sands blow over the ruins of churches he knew in North Africa where the Cross is virtually forbidden. By a blessed irony, a new church is opened every day in formerly Communist Russia, while churches in our own formerly Christian nation are being closed daily. For those who bought into the seductions of politicians' false hopes, there is the counsel of Walt Kelly's character Pogo: "It's always darkest before it goes pitch black."

It is incorrect to say that the coming election poses a choice between two evils. For ethical and aesthetic reasons, there may be some bad in certain candidates, but badness consists in doing bad things. Evil is different: it is the deliberate destruction of truth, virtue, and holiness.

While one may pragmatically vote for a flawed candidate, one may not vote for anyone who advocates and enables unmitigatedly evil acts, and that includes abortion. "In the case of an intrinsically unjust law, such as a law permitting abortion or euthanasia, it is therefore never licit to obey it, or to 'take part in a propaganda campaign in favor of such a law, or vote for it.'"[17]

At one party's convention, the name of God was excluded from its platform, and a woman who boasted of having aborted her child was applauded.[18] It is a grave sin, requiring sacramental confession and pen-

---

[17] St. John Paul II, Encyclical *Evangelium Vitae*, March 25, 1995, no. 73.

[18] The Democratic National Convention held in Philadelphia, July 25 to 28, 2016, nominated former First Lady Hillary Clinton, a vocal supporter of abortion and of Planned Parenthood Federation, for president.

The previous week in Cleveland, July 18 to 21, the Republican National Convention, by contrast, nominated New York entrepreneur Donald J. Trump, who had spoken against abortion during the campaign and vowed to nominate Supreme Court justices "in the mold of [pro-life] Justice Antonin Scalia." The RNC program also included numerous mentions of God by political speakers, as well as formal prayers by religious

ance, to become an accomplice in objective evil by voting for anyone who encourages it, for that imperils the nation and destroys the soul.

It is also the duty of the clergy to make this clear and not to shrink, under the pretense of charity, from explaining the Church's censures. Wolves in sheep's clothing are dangerous, but worse are wolves in shepherd's clothing. While the evils foreseen eight years ago were realized, worse would come if those affronts to human dignity were endorsed again. In the most adverse prospect, God forbid, there might not be another free election, and soon Catholics would arrive at shuttered churches and vacant altars.

The illusion of indifference cannot long be perpetuated by lame jokes and synthetic laughter at banquets, for there is handwriting on the wall.

October 30, 2016

---

leaders—Catholic, Protestant, Eastern Orthodox, Jewish, Sikh, and Muslim.

How to Wage a Just War, Spiritually

L ast week I listed the classical criteria for a just war. While human wars come and go, the spiritual warfare within the soul is never-ending. While there are many terrorists of many kinds, the Terrorist behind all terrorists is the Devil himself. His clever strategy has been to get us to look away from him by persuading us that he does not exist. How many times recently has he almost persuaded us that "character doesn't matter"? The best way to thwart the Devil is to confess sins. Apply the just-war criteria to the spiritual battle this way:

- *The cause must be just.* There is no more just cause than to overcome evil.
- *The war must be directed by a legitimate authority.* Christ gave the Catholic Church the power to forgive sins by giving St. Peter the keys of Heaven and Hell.
- *The intention must be noble.* Our intention is the noblest: to become saints in the service of Christ and His Church.
- *All other means of resolving the conflict must have been exhausted.* Well, every philosophical and psychological and social attempt to fight the Devil has been tried, some more successfully than others, but only confession has eradicated the Terrorist himself by absolving sin.
- *The resulting good must be greater than the damage caused by the war.* Salvation is a good, incalculably preferable to the sacrifices we have to make in overcoming habits and vices.
- *There must be a reasonable chance of success.* Christ guaranteed success over sin and death by rising from the dead and breathing

the Holy Spirit upon the apostles, giving them the power to forgive sins, which power is passed to us through the apostolic succession of the bishops.

· *The ultimate goal must be peace.* The Risen Lord said, "Peace," and that peace we share in the Eucharist and, by God's grace, we will have forever in Heaven.

The most intelligent way to help in our nation's war to protect civilization is by going to confession to protect our souls. The Terrorist does not want us to do it, and that is good enough reason to do it. Jesus wants us to do it, which is an even better reason.

October 21, 2001

ELECTIONS AND THE LAWS OF GOD

Patriotism is related to the virtue of piety, which is reverence for one's ancestors and the truths of one's inheritance. Civil duties, including voting, are binding on the Christian. In his history of the popes, Leopold von Ranke points out that the distinction between sacred and secular powers was a unique insight of Christianity. The separation of the Church from the state was intended to free religion from the civil power. This does not mean that the Christian is not to be involved in the life of the state, nor does it mean that the state is to be run without obedience to God. In the encyclical *Immortale Dei*, Pope Leo XIII said that rulers must set God before them as "their exemplar and law in the administration of the State."

As Election Day approaches, we must reject any facetious concept of "respecting" the laws of God without obeying them. And we must not let a lot of secondary, or prudential issues, be insinuated into the national debate as a smokescreen for violating essential moral norms. While there is latitude for different conscientious positions on war, immigration, capital punishment, tax structures, and the like, there are five issues in this election that are nonnegotiable, and the faithful Catholic must not vote to support them: abortion, euthanasia, embryonic stem-cell research, human cloning, and homosexual "marriage."

As times change, so do the platforms of political parties. It may be difficult to change voting patterns when one has long been a member of a political party. Conscience demands that principles take precedent over custom. Too many Catholics have been guided by habit instead of piety. It is a sin to cooperate materially or formally with the promotion of intrinsically evil acts in the public forum.

Material cooperation would include voting for any candidate who defends abortion and related offenses against human life. Formal cooperation is worse: deliberately voting for such individuals because they take that position. This is not an instruction in whom to vote for. It is an instruction in how to vote according to a formed conscience. If we offend these truths, we eat and drink the Holy Eucharist to our own condemnation (1 Cor. 11:29).

If a politician promotes or defends a political party's platform that violates essential moral norms while boasting that he is a Catholic, and that he once was an altar boy, or some other such fatuity, he brings a grave judgment on himself. The bishops have issued a check-off list of the positions of the major presidential candidates. Without endorsing any particular candidate, they indicate that President Bush is consistent with the Church's moral teaching on the five basic issues, while Senator Kerry is not. Consequently, Senator Kerry is the first presidential candidate officially to be endorsed by Planned Parenthood. It is the duty of every pastor to advise the faithful of these facts.

October 24, 2004

Science and Catholics

Analysis of a tomb in St. Paul Outside-the-Walls, commissioned by the Pope four years ago, using carbon-14 and DNA analysis, enabled the announcement earlier this year that it does indeed contain the remains of St. Paul. Similarly, computer analysis has now verified the discovery of the long-lost body of Mikolaj Kopernik (1473–1543), popularly known as Nicolaus Copernicus, buried anonymously in the Polish cathedral of Frombork. DNA samples of a femur bone and a tooth matched the DNA of a strand of hair found in one of his books in a Swedish library. Digital reconstruction from his skull done in a crime lab reproduced his broken nose and a scar on the forehead.

Copernicus, son of a Polish father and a German mother, was a priest and the temporary administrator of the diocese of Frauenburg. As a Renaissance man, he put Leonardo da Vinci in the shade, although painting seems to be the one art that did not claim him as a master. After studies in the universities of Krakow (where Pope John Paul II studied and taught), Bologna, Padua, and Ferrara, he became a prominent jurist and mathematician and also practiced medicine for six years, donating his service to the poor. The polymath pioneered reform of the monetary system as it was developing in his day and did it so well that he was made an economic adviser to the government of Prussia. In what little spare time he had, he translated into Latin for posterity the Greek letters of Theophylactus.

He studied astronomy well enough to lecture in Rome on the planets, and shortly before his death he completed his heliocentric cosmology. This "Copernican Revolution," which overturned the Ptolemaic picture of Earth as the center of the universe—except for Manhattan, of course—launched modern astronomy and greatly influenced Galileo, who was born twenty-one years after the death of Copernicus. He was too careful a theologian to muddle astronomy with astrology, as did Galileo, nor did he insist unscientifically that his theory was absolute fact, a mistake that got Galileo into trouble.

Father Copernicus seems to have been so self-effacing that he was not considered well-known enough for a marked grave. He did not change the world, as Christ did, but he changed the way the world is understood. He stands in the line of such Catholic scientists as Pascal the mathematician; Lavoisier the father of modern chemistry; Schrodinger the discoverer of wave mechanics; Vesalius the anatomist; Fermi the creator of atomic physics; Malphigi, who developed microscopic anatomy; von Neumann, who theorized the modern computer; the childless monk Mendel, who became the father of genetics; Pasteur, whose germ theory saved countless lives; and Fleming, whose penicillin probably saved more lives than any other discovery in history. The identification of the body of Copernicus is a fitting reminder of this great and continuing tradition.

October 25, 2009

WORTHILY TO THE FEAST

As a priest, I have witnessed the marriages of more than eight hundred couples. It is gratifying to hear from them on their anniversaries, and to baptize and even marry some of their new generation. Solid marriages are beacons and ballast for those whose understanding of family life may be dim and unsettled in our distressed culture. Some of the happiest weddings have been free of the extravagance that is the fashion of a meretricious society. Sometimes, a couple prayerfully decides to call the wedding off, and usually this is prudent, if it is the outcome of an awareness of the seriousness of the vows.

The other day a couple in California called off their wedding, having already paid for a $35,000 reception. Rather than cancel, the family invited the homeless of Sacramento to share the feast. Young and old and abandoned showed up, and what could have been a dismal day—something like Miss Havisham's cobwebbed banquet table with its desiccated wedding cake—became bright for many.

That brought to mind the 1987 Danish film *Babettes gæstebud*, which as *Babette's Feast* won an Academy Award for Best Foreign Language Film. In a snowy village on the west coast of Jutland, home to a graying small group who belong to a rigid Pietistic sect, a kindly woman arrives from Paris and volunteers to serve as cook for two elderly sisters whose father had founded their conventicle. Fourteen years pass, during which Babette Hersant cooks the bland meals that are the customary fare of the villagers. Then one day she announces that, in honor of what would have been the father's hundredth birthday, she will prepare a feast.

The villagers are suspicious that such luxury might be some form of devilry, so they decide to pretend that they are unfazed by the repast. Babette's secret is that she has won ten thousand francs in a lottery and spent it all on delicacies delivered from France. As the dinner proceeds, barriers built by festering resentments break down, and the astringency of the people gives way to reminiscences of their romantic youth. Babette remains in the village happily penniless, because "an artist is never poor."

If Eucharistic metaphors in the plot may be stretched by belabored eisegesis,[19] the original story by Karen Blixen, who ironically died from malnutrition, echoes the parable of "The Marriage of the King's Son." Those who were first invited had excuses, so the king's servants gathered in all they could find in the streets. One of the invitees is cast out for not wearing a wedding garment. God's gratuitousness, by its very munificence, requires a change of heart.

The required "state of grace" for Holy Communion has been debated at the recent synod in Rome. What is clear is that the Wedding Feast of the Lamb is offered to all, but the invitation requires a humble submission to the king's heavenly protocol.

October 25, 2015

---

[19] According to Merriam-Webster, eisegesis is "the interpretation of a text (as of the Bible) by reading into it one's own ideas."

PRAYER FOR A NEW NATION

Today a long-forgotten crucifix will be placed once again in the Basilica of St. Peter in Rome. It will hang in the Blessed Sacrament Chapel near Bernini's great tabernacle. Bernini himself would have admired the work of the anonymous artist, for its medieval style anticipated the spirit of the more exuberant baroque.

The crucifix was carved seven hundred years ago and was the object of devotion in the original Constantinian basilica, built in the fourth century. The torso and legs are seven feet long and are in one piece made from the trunk of a walnut tree. It was placed in the new basilica in 1626 and survived many vicissitudes, including the Sack of Rome, when the invaders used the old basilica as a horse stable and mockingly vested the corpus in one of their uniforms.

Gradually, it was forgotten after it was removed to make room for Michelangelo's *Pietà* and ended up in a remote and virtually unreachable chapel. High technology has restored it, as it suffered discoloration and termite damage. The sort of stereo microscopes used in microsurgery identified the many layers of paint and varnish before they were meticulously removed.

The outstretched arms are six and a half feet wide. Even if the Lord had not been nailed to the Cross, His arms would be open to all who approach Him, as they were when He ascended into glory. "Come unto me, all you that labor and are heavy laden, and I will give you rest" (Matt. 11:28).

Our nation is weary, and the ennui is especially taxing and belabored by a long election campaign. Events have forced us to examine the condition of our culture, and how much we have ignored Christ's call to come to Him. The degradation of our institutions, reflected tellingly even in the way people dress and speak, is palpable and has taken its toll on our schools and governments and even our churches. This is a time, rarely matched in our national annals, for choosing between conversion and tragedy. To choose the tragic path is to mock Our Lord, and our demoralized culture is already well on its way to masquerading Christ Crucified in comic vestments.

Two hundred twenty-five years ago, to this very week, Bishop John Carroll penned a prayer for the new nation. As the first bishop in the United States, cousin of a signer of the Declaration of Independence and an esteemed friend of many Founding Fathers, he stood on a terrain high enough to survey the looming dangers and salutary prospects of the day, as he prayed for a government "encouraging due respect for virtue and religion; by a faithful execution of the laws in justice and mercy; and by restraining vice and immorality." Our perspective is the same today, only with more souls both at risk and offered benevolent promise.

November 6, 2016

NOT FOR EARTH, BUT ETERNITY

Although city parishes are not commonly thought of as "family oriented" the way suburban parishes are, and while urban conditions make it costly and difficult to rear children, it is gratifying to welcome a steadily increasing number of families to our parish and to baptize the children of couples married here. Pope Leo XIII called the family "the cradle of civil society" and said that the destiny of states is largely fostered in the circle of family life.

As a reminder of the sanctity of the family as the "little church" or *ecclesiola*, last Sunday the Church beatified the parents of St. Thérèse of Lisieux, who was canonized in 1925. Beatification is the last degree before canonization. The ceremony took place in the basilica of Lisieux, according to the preferred practice of Pope Benedict to have the beatification rite in the place where the blessed ones lived. Louis and Zélie Martin were not beatified because their daughter is a famous saint. Their own heroic virtue was attested by a miracle required in the beatification process: in this case, their intercession healed a man's malformed lung. Their earthly lives were outwardly ordinary, typical of a French bourgeois family in the nineteenth century. Louis was a prosperous watchmaker. He had wanted to be a monk, and needed the counsel of a priest to explain the sanctity of fatherhood. He and Zélie were married in Alençon in 1858 and never ceased exchanging love letters. Five of their nine children joined religious orders. Their daughter St. Thérèse wrote, "The good God gave me a father and a mother more worthy of heaven than of earth." After Zélie's death, Louis worked hard to care for his children with a contagious happiness.

There has been a widespread breakdown of family life in our society due to many reasons, including a loss of a sense of the holiness of marriage, worsened by government policies that threaten family stability. It is widely recognized that welfare programs begun in the 1960s backfired in their attempt to help children. Today this is worsened by civil attempts to redefine marriage against the natural law. Nonetheless, there is a desire on the part of many not to repeat the mistakes of the past. Many young couples have learned the importance of families the hard way, often through the failures of the last generation. In one recent five-year period for which there are statistics, couples with three or more children increased from 11.4 percent to 18.4 percent.

It may take a long time to repair the damage done to society by misguided social engineers who scorned the traditional family, but the Church lives by the vision expressed by Pope Pius XI at a time when a fascist government tried to usurp the role of parents: "The family is more sacred than the state, and men are begotten not for the earth and for time, but for heaven and eternity."[20]

October 26, 2008

---

[20] Pope Pius XI, Encyclical *Casti Connubii*, December 31, 1930, no. 69.

Strings Attached

"He who pays the piper calls the tune" is a saying based on the Scottish custom of having the lord of the manor choose the music for which he is paying. Sometimes in lieu of money, the piper was given a dram of whisky in a bowl called a *quaich* (pronounced "quake"), and the liquor was often referred to as "lucre." If you are in someone's pay, he will tell you what to do.

This has long been a challenge when the Church accepts the patronage of a civil ruler. St. Athanasius and St. John Chrysostom stood up to such emperors as Julian the Apostate and Theodosius, who were outspoken in what they thought was their right to call the tune. After the Great Schism, the Byzantine Church had an even greater problem with this "Caesaropapism," since it no longer had a protector in the Pope. And the problem pertains even today in the new post-Soviet Russian government. In the West as well, St. Ambrose and St. Hilary of Poitiers had to face down civil rulers. Pope Gregory VII kept the emperor Henry IV waiting in the snow. Pius VI and VII fared worse with the emperor Napoleon.

In the eighteenth century, the Holy Roman Emperor Joseph II was called the "Sacristan of Europe" because, although he was something of a religious skeptic, he regulated all the details of worship, even to the design of candlesticks, and censored the contents of sermons. In this he was something like Annise Parker, the mayor of Houston, who caused a stir recently with her subpoena of the sermons of five local clergymen on the grounds that Christian expressions might violate the city's Equal Rights Ordinance. The emperor Joseph II might have admired her moxy, although the protocols of his court would have been confused if she had visited with the woman she calls her "wife." The Texas attorney general called her subpoena "a direct assault on the religious liberty granted by the First Amendment."

There is a logic to governments giving grants to charities run by religious institutions, since they run the charities more efficiently than the government. In two recent years, Catholic Church agencies received 1.5 billion dollars in grants. But the piper may call the tune. Some Catholic hospitals already have had to close rather than do the government's dance. Consider a case in Idaho, where city officials have told clergymen that they must officiate at same-sex weddings, or face fines of $1,000 a day and time in jail. Then there is the neuralgic fact of tax exemptions. Chief Justice John Marshall's decision in *McCulloch v. Maryland* (1819) paraphrased the defense of Daniel Webster: "The power to tax is the power to destroy."

It all boils down to rendering unto Caesar and unto God. Christ expected the Pharisees of His day to know the difference. He expects the same of us.

October 26, 2014

WITNESSES

One of the most joyful songs for entering a church building is Psalm 122, which begins: "I was glad when they said unto me, let us go into the house of the Lord." And there is no more transportingly beautiful setting for it than that composed by Sir Charles Hubert Hastings Parry. Whatever may be the quality of a church's architecture, it is made beautiful by the Presence of the Lord, accompanied by the silent witness of the angels and saints. I am grateful that there seems to be an increasing number of worshippers coming to the churches for which I am responsible, and I am especially thankful for the care that so many show for them.

Recently, a group of volunteers formed to help clean the heavily trafficked Church of the Holy Innocents. I would say that not only does it make the church more suitable for worship, but that the very acts of sweeping and scrubbing and polishing can themselves be forms of prayer, quite as St. Teresa of Avila said that she prayed while scrubbing pots and pans. As the Jews, including Our Lord, sang as they climbed the steps to the Temple, so may we sing, "Our feet shall stand within thy gates, O Jerusalem." Whether the people enter St. Michael's from Thirty-Fourth Street or Holy Innocents from Thirty-Seventh Street, they really do find themselves in touch with the Heavenly Jerusalem, of which the earthly city is a cipher and a sign.

In preparation for the great days of All Saints and All Souls, the faithful should keep constantly in mind the witnesses who have gone before us. On Monday, October 28, Mass will be offered in the Church of the Holy Innocents in honor of Blessed Karl of Austria, who, although the last emperor of Austria and the last king of Hungary, is a quite modern saint, whose family are still around and known to some of us. Blessed Karl's life reminds a culture deprived of great leaders that spiritual greatness can still be achieved through, and not in spite of, positions of political authority. Blessed Karl was a model of the true peacemaker, not content with the sort of tenuous peace fabricated by compromise with evil, but insistent on the true peace "which passes all understanding" and that only humble obedience to Christ can give.

Lighting a candle, sweeping a church floor, kneeling as Christ comes to the altar are various acts in the holy house of the same God of those who gladly climb the steps of His house to kneel before Him, and of those who unthinkingly walk past, absorbed in matters that seem important only for the passing moment. Whatever may be lacking in our song, the saints and angels supply: "Pray for the peace of Jerusalem: they shall prosper that love thee."

October 27, 2013

"Are These the Men?"

I have enjoyed reviewing some of our neighborhood history and am especially mindful of the fateful day in 1776, on September 15, when the Revolutionary War almost was concluded here. This parish was mostly meadows and some swampland, and the streets as we know them did not exist. George Washington, up around what we now call 100th Street, could hear the cannons as the British troops landed at present-day 34th Street. There they captured more than three hundred American troops and about twenty officers. This was discouraging since more than fourteen hundred American soldiers already had been killed in the Battle of Long Island. General Washington galloped down here, to find his soldiers fleeing in panic. He positioned himself on horseback where the Grand Hyatt and Chrysler buildings now stand.

Famous for that composure and *gravitas* the ancient Romans esteemed in their leaders, Washington in that moment dashed his hat to the ground and began to strike the fleeing men with the broadside of his sword: foot soldiers and officers, even one brigadier general. They refused his orders to dig in and fight. Finally he cried in righteous fury: "Are these the men with whom I am to save America?"

As a regiment of Hessians neared, a young aide-de-camp pulled Washington's horse away by the bridle, and the great man finally withdrew to Harlem Heights, moments from capture. Soon Aaron Burr secretly led five thousand troops up the west side of Manhattan, and the Americans prevailed. For days, General Howe had the British and Hessian soldiers encamp on what is our church property.

We are now engaged in another war. Washington was a great man, but Christ is more than great, and His divine voice summons us, in New York as once in Galilee: "When the Son of Man comes, will he find any faith on the earth?" (Luke 18:8). If Washington tested his men with his sword, Our Lord tests our faith in other ways. St. Augustine said, "When the Lord sought me I hid from Him, and when I sought Him, He hid from me." Faith, as a gift to the intellect accepted by a free will and increased by grace, teaches us that God does not fail us, and that the climactic battle of life—the one for the salvation of souls—is certain of victory for those who have faith.

October 28, 2001

THE DESIRE TO GIVE

The canonization of Marianne Cope, along with Kateri Tekakwitha, on October 21, occasioned the publication of a stunning photograph showing Marianne standing beside the funeral bier of St. Damien in Kalaupapa, Molokai. That was in 1889, and the picture is so sharp that it could have been taken today. It must be the first photograph of two saints together. The holy friendships of Teresa of Avila with John of the Cross, and Francis de Sales with Jane de Chantal illuminated civilization before photography.

St. Damien's body is scarred with leprosy but vested in the fine chasuble in which he used to offer Mass. St. Marianne, in her timeless religious habit, shows no sorrow, for she obviously knows she is looking at a saint, not knowing that she is one herself.

Studying that photograph, one thinks of how hard they worked, not only among the outcast lepers, but all their lives. Damien, born Jozef De Veuster in Belgium, was a farm boy, and Marianne left school in Utica, New York, after the eighth grade to support her family by working in factories.

Not in the picture was their helper, Joseph Dutton, a Civil War veteran who was so traumatized by the ravages of war and his broken marriage that he became an alcoholic. He reformed his life, went to Molokai, and worked with the lepers for forty-five years—cleaning latrines, scrubbing floors, and binding sores—until his death in 1931. Their great happiness would have been clouded to see how much unhappiness there is in our land today.

As a typical eighteenth-century rationalist, Edward Gibbon was cynical about Christianity, but as a historian he analyzed the staying power of civilizations in terms of natural virtue: "That public virtue, which among the ancients was denominated patriotism, is derived from a strong sense of our own interest in the preservation and prosperity of the free government of which we are members. Such a sentiment, which had rendered the legions of the Republic almost invincible, could make but a very feeble impression on the mercenary servants of a despotic prince."[21]

And as England's Prime Minister Margaret Thatcher pointed out, when the people's deepest desire becomes security, rather than freedom, wanting "not to give to society, but for society to give to them," they lose both their security and their freedom.[22]

I expect that Gibbon would have understood modern saints no better than he did the early martyrs and confessors, but he would have seen in them a selfless energy that builds noble societies, and the neglect of such energy pulls them down. Our own nation is facing these realities as it decides what it wants to be. The present crisis in culture cannot be resolved if it is addressed only in terms of economics and international relations. The real leaders are not those who hypnotize naïve people into thinking that they are the source of hope. Those who can rescue nations from servility to selfishness are not on slick campaign posters, but in stark black and white photographs like that taken on Molokai in 1889.

October 28, 2012

---

[21] Edward Gibbon, *The History of the Decline and Fall of the Roman Empire*, vol. 1, pt. 2, chap. 1.

[22] Lady Margaret Thatcher, "The Moral Foundations of Society," lecture at The Hillsdale Center for Constructive Alternatives seminar, "God and Man: Perspectives on Christianity in the 20th Century (1994).

POLITICS VERSUS FAITH AND REASON

Not everyone in history has had, or has, the precious privilege of electing their leaders and shaping their government. Despite all its defects, the democratic system has been secured for us at great sacrifice over the generations, and vigil must constantly be kept for its integrity. In 1999, the bishops of the United States reiterated the Church's teaching on voting as a duty: "For Catholics, public virtue is as important as private virtue in building up the common good. In the Catholic tradition, responsible citizenship is a virtue; participation in the political process is a moral obligation." As another Election Day nears, I recall a recent instruction on this written by His Eminence Francis Cardinal George, archbishop of Chicago, as he addressed the role of conscience in political matters. Conscience is to be *formed*, which means that it is to be instructed by the moral norms and should not be an excuse for acting irrationally.

Although principles are clear, problems result in their practical application because of confusion of priorities and the temptations of self-interest. In all public considerations, the first interest must be the dignity of every human person and the right to life. As a natural law, this can be understood and affirmed by non-Christians. The Catholic must know, from the Church's moral system, that Catholic politicians must not compromise conscience under the excuse of not "imposing doctrine on others." The protection of innocent life is rational and not only doctrinal, although the two go together. For example, the prohibition against stealing as a sin is a doctrinal precept, but it also is rationally understood as an essential element in the common good. Our present legal system is irrational, as it protects "stocks and bonds, as well as dogs and cats" more carefully than it protects unborn human beings.[23]

It is offensive to God and conscience to neglect moral principles in order to vote for a particular political party or candidate out of custom. Many politicians advertise themselves as Catholic, or as friendly to the Church, and then hold Catholic moral principles in contempt. It is only the ignorance or self-interest of Catholic voters that keeps these misrepresentative representatives in office.

Cardinal George writes: "In the long run, God governs creation and the ideals of Catholic social doctrine are therefore possible of accomplishment. In the short run, we have to vote.... It's important to vote in a democratic society, even though much of our life is governed by decisions of unelected bureaucrats and judges and editors and economic players whose names we do not recognize unless there is a scandal of some sort. May each of us do the best we can, using the dialogue between faith and reason that takes place in our hearts, guided by the Church's social doctrine; and may God protect us and our country."[24]

October 29, 2006

[23] Cardinal Francis E. George, O.M.I., "Religion, Reason, Voting," *Catholic New World*, October 15, 2006, posted at https://www.catholicculture.org/.
[24] Ibid.

OUR ONE PURPOSE

The reason for being a Christian is to be a saint, for a saint is a human who is fully human according to the intention of Christ. November 1, the feast of All Saints, is both the proof that Christianity works (for there are countless saints) and the inspiration for us to keep trying. It is a Holy Day of Obligation, but "obligation" is a weak and begrudging term for any holy day. These holy days are immense gifts to us from Heaven, reminding us of why we are alive. In 834, Pope Gregory IV moved the feast of all the martyrs (eventually to include all the saints) from May 13 to November 1 — as if, by some unconscious prophecy, May 13 would be reserved to celebrate the apparitions of Our Lady of Fatima nearly eleven hundred years later.

As Christmas sanctified the pagan Roman feast of Saturnalia, so All Saints' Day would sanctify the pagan Druid feast of Samhain ("Sowen"), the Lord of the Dead, on which the Celtic people from Ireland to Brittany had marked their new year and the beginning of winter. Some explanations for customs we have inherited may or may not be fanciful. It does seem that the Romans added to the Celtic customs their own drinking of cider and apple-bobbing for the goddess of orchards, Pomona (later to spread her name to California). But these were not jolly feasts.

Paganism suffered the melancholy of knowing about death but not knowing of the resurrection of the dead. Pagan feasts easily turned into macabre grotesqueries and orgiastic debauches out of despair. Our neo-pagan culture has reverted to that, but you cannot go back to sturdy old paganism; you can only update its remnant sadness. Halloween, properly the vigil of All Hallows' Day, has become more popular than All Saints' itself. Some denominations even advertise Halloween festivals in their churches, with spooky music and haunting images, in a deluded attempt to attract people they cannot attract to celebrate holiness. There is nothing wrong with innocent fun, but it can be a sign that people who once were Christian are haunted by their loss of faith.

All Saints' Day is followed by All Souls' Day—when the Church prays for the blessed ones who have been judged by God as worthy to join the saints in glory in God's good time. The *Catechism* says, "A perennial link of charity exists between the faithful who have already reached their heavenly home, those who are expiating their sins in purgatory, and those who are still pilgrims on earth. Between them there is, too, an abundant exchange of all good things" (no. 1475).[25]

October 27, 2002

---

[25] Quoting *Indulgentiarum doctrina*, 5.

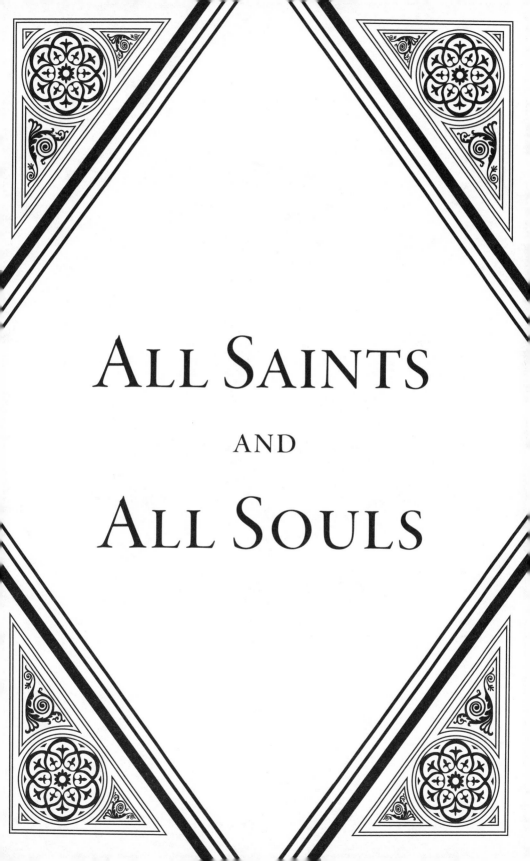

ALL SAINTS

AND

ALL SOULS

No Dead Saints

The expression "a living saint" can be misleading. Certainly, we have encountered people in our lives who fit that description, as best as we can judge. The Holy Church makes the final decision about saints. We celebrate them especially on All Saints' Day; and on All Souls' Day, we pray for our loved ones who are drawing more closely into the aura of holiness. The saints on the calendar are only the tip of the iceberg, and most of the saints who have ever existed are known to God alone. Perhaps churches should have a shrine to "The Unknown Saint" quite as we have a Tomb of the Unknown Soldier. All Saints' Day is rather like that.

My point, though, is that there is no such thing as a dead saint. There are saints alive now, and there are saints who have physically died, but all are alive in Christ, and they are "busy" in heaven, to use a temporal metaphor. Some saints capture the popular imagination more in one generation than in another. For instance, St. Simon Stylites was admired in Syria in the fifth century for spending most of his life seated on top of a pillar. That is not a useful model for our day, although some may still remember Flagpole Kelly, and not long ago thousands of New Yorkers went to watch a man spend a week on top of a column up the street in Bryant Park.

Millions are drawn to Padre Pio, and some are compelled by an unmeasured fascination with his miraculous spiritual gifts, which were blessings indeed, rather than emulating his heroic humility and discipline. There remains an astonishing cult of St. Thérèse of Lisieux. She was almost the reverse of St. Pio: totally unknown in her earthly lifetime, and accomplishing nothing conspicuous to her contemporaries. She would have remained such had not her spiritual writings been discovered and published. Perhaps she fascinates precisely because in just barely twenty-four years on earth, she did the most ordinary things with most extraordinary joy. Whenever her relics are taken on pilgrimage to foreign lands (not to mention the one that was taken on a space shuttle), hundreds of thousands pour out to pray by them. This happened most recently in England, where the media were confounded by the huge crowds.

Concurrent with that phenomenon, there were astonishing developments in long-moribund Christian life there, not least of which was the announcement of the first papal state visit to Britain and the expected beatification of John Henry Newman, who predicted a "Second Spring" of Faith in England. Then came news of an Apostolic Constitution, which will provide a unique canonical structure to welcome those desiring union with the Catholic Church. Pope Benedict XVI, who well deserves the title "The Pope of Unity," has shown the power of the intercessions of the saints.

November 1, 2009

"I Looked Back and Saw My Father"

Even in New York City, nature does not go unnoticed. Though we do not get to see much of the autumnal leaves, the sharpening winds over the river and the honking of migrating geese competing with the traffic horns still send the message that the seasons are changing and with them the mood of time. Autumn mixes beauty and melancholy, which is how it must be in a transient world, and why the most beautiful sights and sounds move the spirit beyond diaphanous pleasure to twinges of a strange longing, like the Jews in the exile of Babylon unable to play their harps while longing for their homeland.

All Saints' Day and All Souls' Day fit well into the autumnal hours, too radiant for laughter and too mysterious for solace. The feast of All Saints this year is on Sunday, and All Souls is its Monday afterglow. Contemplating the eternal life of the blessed ones is more vital than admiring a painting in the Met or music in Carnegie Hall, for the blessed souls of the faithful are urging us to join them, not as a romance but as an utterly possible proposal.

The actress Maureen O'Hara said that she wanted to live to be 102, so that as an old lady she could annoy people by thumping her cane and making peremptory demands. She just died at 95, which is close enough, and that occasioned some autumnal thoughts of my own, for I knew her when she came to Mass and afterward would tell many stories. She favored the sonority of the older form of the Latin Mass, though she worshiped God wherever He tabernacled. After I preached a series of Lenten meditations, she reminisced about my favorite film, *How Green Was My Valley*. It made full use of the novel by Richard Llewellyn and was a triumph of the screen in a time when English speech had not decayed. The concluding reminiscence of his youth in a Welsh mining village is heavy with autumn and light with spring, and makes a descant on what saints and souls sing with perfect pitch:

> I saw behind me those who had gone, and before me, those who were to come. I looked back and saw my father.... Then I was not afraid, for I was in a long line that had no beginning, and no end, and the hand of his father grasped my father's hand, and his hand was in mine, and my unborn son took my right hand, and all, up and down the line that stretched from Time That Was, to Time That Is, and Is Not Yet, raised their hands to show the link, and we found that we were one, born of Woman, Son of Man, made in the Image, fashioned in the Womb by the Will of God, the Eternal Father.

November 1, 2015

PURIFICATION

In the ancient Roman world, a boy at the age of seven was instructed by his father in the virtue of *pietas* (reverence for the gods and ancestors). This, along with derivative virtues, constituted the classical citizen, emblematic of the noble Roman republic—and conspicuously abandoned in the moral decay of the later empire. Piety gained a supernatural character when Christ gave the Church the Holy Spirit. Christian piety becomes reverence for the one true God and communion with the faithful departed through prayer, as we do especially on All Souls' Day.

One way we revere the beloved dead is to apply indulgences for them, just as can be done for the living. "An indulgence is the remission before God of the temporal punishment due to sins whose guilt has already been forgiven, which the faithful Christian who is duly disposed gains under certain prescribed conditions through the action of the Church which, as the minister of redemption, dispenses and applies with authority the treasury of the satisfactions of Christ and the saints."[26]

Indulgences respond to the reality that there are two consequences of sin:

> Grave sin deprives us of communion with God and therefore makes us incapable of eternal life, the privation of which is called the "eternal punishment" of sin. On the other hand, every sin, even venial, entails an unhealthy attachment to creatures, which must be purified either here on earth or after death in the state

---

[26] *Indulgentiarum Doctrina*, 1.

called Purgatory. This purification frees one from what is called the "temporal punishment" of sin. These two punishments must not be conceived of as a kind of vengeance inflicted by God from without, but as following from the very nature of sin. A conversion which proceeds from a fervent charity can attain the complete purification of the sinner in such a way that no punishment would remain. (CCC 1472).

Piety also includes devotion to one's country, for which we should especially pray at this election time. The nearly fifty million babies destroyed by abortion since *Roe v. Wade* do not need prayers for the dead because the Lord has already received them according to His merciful will. But our nation is accountable for allowing this deepest outrage against innocent life to continue and expand. Holy Church has widely published the fact that no one is morally justified in preferring any political candidate who promotes abortion over one who does not. Only the invincibly ignorant can hope to escape severe penalties, eternal as well as temporal, if they reject this counsel. The social philosopher Thomas Sowell has said, "It is hard to think of a time when a nation—and a whole civilization—has drifted more futilely toward a bigger catastrophe than that looming over the United States and Western civilization today.... We are fast approaching the point of no return."[27]

November 2, 2008

---

[27] Thomas Sowell, "Point of No Return?" TownHall, August 22, 2006, https://townhall.com/.

YOUNG PRIESTS, FERVENT PRIESTS

Recently the feasts of the Franciscans St. John of Capistrano, who fought to save Belgrade from an attack by the Ottoman Turks in 1451, and St. Peter of Alcantara, who was a great friend of St. Teresa of Avila, called to mind a cause both of them held dear: the reform of the lives of priests and religious. Before the Council of Trent there were no seminaries, as we know them. These saints worked hard to improve the quality of priestly formation as it then existed. The Church is doing the same now.

A recent *Los Angeles Times* poll of 1,854 younger priests in 80 U.S. dioceses reflects a widespread trend toward more fervent orthodoxy. Clerics under age 41 indicated more loyalty to the Church on dogmatic and moral issues than their elders. By their own description, three-fourths said they were more religiously orthodox than their older counterparts. Nearly 80 percent of them rank His Holiness John Paul II as "outstanding" among the popes, compared with 60 percent of Vatican II–generation priests and 64 percent of pre–Vatican II priests over the age of 60.

The renewal of solid belief and practice after a generation of pick-and-choose "cafeteria Catholicism" goes along with a more optimistic attitude about the future of Catholic life (69 percent see the life of the Church in general as "excellent" or "good" in contrast to 56 percent of the Vatican II generation, which pollsters define as those 42 to 59 years old).

Only 48 percent of younger priests think Roman Catholics can disagree in good faith with some Church teaching, while 72 percent of the older priests thought so. All groups polled ranked moral scandals as the number-one problem facing the Church today. Older priests thought that reforms should include radical changes in the priesthood. The vast majority of younger priests stressed that moral decay is rooted in a neglect of traditional priestly standards and contempt for orthodox belief.

Dioceses that most clearly follow orthodox patterns have the most priestly vocations. One example is the Diocese of Lincoln, Nebraska, with a Catholic population of only 90,000. It has two rapidly growing new seminaries and three new orders of nuns, including a new Carmelite monastery of cloistered women established last September. The vicar-general of Lincoln, Monsignor Timothy Thorburn, says that the national priest shortage is "a short-term problem" that will be solved in a few decades by the return to orthodoxy. He says, "Young people with ideals are not looking for the easy path. A 'Catholic lite' is not attractive to them."[28] St. John of Capistrano and St. Peter of Alcantara would understand.

November 3, 2002

[28] Teresa Watanabe, "Young Priests Hold Old Values," *Los Angeles Times*, October 21, 2002, http://articles.latimes.com/.

BLESSED EMPEROR

May our two splendid parishes, Holy Innocents in the Garment District and St. Michael in Hell's Kitchen (gradually becoming Heaven's Kitchen), grow ever closer in strengthening their witness to the power of the Resurrection. In these days of the octave of All Saints, do bear in mind that countless saints, mostly unknown, have walked through these troubled and challenging streets. Last Monday His Excellency Dom Teodoro de Faria, bishop emeritus of Funchal, on Portugal's Island of Madeira, celebrated Holy Mass at the altar of the Church of the Holy Innocents. It was in his diocese that Blessed Karl von Habsburg, the last emperor of Austria-Hungary, died. With today's medicine, Blessed Karl might well have survived the pneumonia that afflicted him, but instead he died at the age of thirty-four in penurious exile, a victim of the bigotry of many, including—sad to say—our own country's Calvinist president Woodrow Wilson.

The novelist Anatole France said, "No one will ever persuade me that the war could not have been ended long ago. The Emperor Charles offered peace. There is the only honest man who occupied an important position during the war, but he was not listened to."[29]

Blessed Charles, beatified by Pope John Paul II, whose father had served under him and who bore the emperor's name, was shocked to inherit the imperial throne, as he was remote in the line of succession.

---

[29] Quoted by Sir Charles Petrie, *Twenty Years' Armistice and After: British Foreign Policy Since 1918* (London: Eyre and Spottiswoode, 1940), 12.

It was the worst time in history, and by the end of the First World War, more than half of his fellow countrymen had died in battle. In his brief two years of reign, Charles instituted many reforms of the army and the nation, even using imperial carriages to transport food and fuel to the poor, modeling himself after the social teachings of Pope Leo XIII.

His love was boundless for his wife, the empress Zita, whom he told on the day after their glittering wedding, "Now we must help each other to get to Heaven." His feast day is not on the anniversary of his death or his birth, but on the anniversary of their wedding. In cruel exile after the war, he was not allowed firewood, and the family shivered in the cold on the island of Madeira. Before his death, Charles blessed his eighth child, still in the empress's womb, young enough legally to be "eliminated" in our present society. The young father was reluctant to let his eldest son, Otto, who would be a principal figure in the collapse of European communism, watch him die but said that he must see how a Christian king goes to God.

The empress and her eight children removed to various lands, most recently living in Tuxedo Park in our own archdiocese. In Quebec they were so neglected that she had to comb the public park for dandelions to feed the royal family.

We rejoice in the heroism of these saints and pray that, whatever our state in life, we may serve the King of the Universe as they did.

November 3, 2013

AMONG WOLVES

Considering how many crucial matters were at stake during the recent election, including the right to life and religious freedom, and the preponderant bias in the media and opinion polls, it did not seem melodramatic to hope for a prudential hand to guide things. There will be much thanksgiving on Thanksgiving Day.

Some who trusted pundits were shocked that their perception was an illusion, confirming T. S. Eliot's words in his "Four Quartets": "Humankind cannot bear very much reality." The *New York Times*, fearful of further declines in its dropping influence, apologized for misreading the demographics of our culture and came as close as it could to admitting that it had been wrong, by confessing that it had not been right. But thousands accustomed to life in a parallel universe and impervious to the rebukes of reason expressed their befuddlement at the results of the presidential election by demonstrating and even rioting when facts shattered their expectations.

Our college campuses have been breeding grounds for self-absorption and corruption of the senses. Professors who had never attained moral maturity themselves reacted by providing "safe spaces" for students traumatized by reality. In universities across the land, by a sodality of silliness in the academic establishment, these "safe spaces" were supplied with soft cushions, hot chocolate, coloring books, and attendant psychologists. At least one university provided friendly kittens and puppies for weeping students to cuddle. A college chaplaincy invited students to pray, the implication being that their petitions might persuade the Lord to rethink His political leanings.

The average age of a Continental soldier in the American Revolution was one year less than that of a college freshman today. Alexander Hamilton was a fighting lieutenant general at twenty-one, not to mention Joan of Arc, who led an army into battle and saved France when she was about as old as an American college sophomore. In our Civil War, eight Union generals and seven Confederate generals were under the age of twenty-five. The age of most U.S. and RAF fighter pilots in World War II was about that of those on college junior-varsity teams. Catholics who hoped in this election for another Lepanto miracle will remember that back in 1571, Don Juan of Austria saved Western civilization as commanding admiral when he was twenty-four. None of these figures, in the various struggles against the world and the flesh and evil, retreated to safe spaces, weeping in the arms of grief therapists.

What will the frightened half adults do when they leave their safe spaces and enter a society where there is no one to offer them hot chocolate? Christ formed His disciples in a more practical way: "I am sending you out like sheep among wolves. Therefore, be as shrewd as snakes and as innocent as doves" (Matt. 10:16). We are here today because those disciples did as they were told, and were not shrewd as doves and innocent as snakes.

November 20, 2016

PROPHECY TODAY

Prophets are sometimes thought of as fortune-tellers. Fortune-telling is actually a serious sin, if it is taken seriously, because it denies the freedom to choose what will become of us. To "choose your fate" is a contradiction in terms, because fate rules out free choice. Human beings are not victims of fate. They are children of providence. Prophets got the reputation of foretelling events only because they declared the will of God, and by so doing they were able to lay before human logic the consequences of rejecting that divine will. The belief in providence is one of the radical differences between Judeo-Christianity and Islam, which believes in fated destiny, or *kismet*.

St. John the Baptist was the last and greatest of the old-style prophets. There has been no need for prophecy since God revealed Himself in Christ, "The Word was made flesh." However, the prophetic office of the Church continues, as the job of explaining what has already been revealed. No longer is it necessary to foretell the Messiah, so the prophet is now the reflective teacher, and any thoughtful Christian can anticipate at least in general terms what will happen when the truth of Christ is accepted or rejected. In that sense, two of the most prophetic voices in the twentieth century were the English journalist G. K. Chesterton and his friend the popular historian Hilaire Belloc. For starters, consider these comments:

In his newspaper column for the *Illustrated London News* exactly ninety years ago today (November 4, 1911), Chesterton wrote:

A good Moslem king was one who was strict in religion, valiant in battle, just in giving judgment among his people, but not one who had the slightest objection in international matters to removing his neighbour's landmark.

Then there is this a few years later in Belloc's book *The Great Heresies*:

Today we are accustomed to think of the Mohammedan world as something backward and stagnant, in all material affairs at least, but not so very long ago, less than a hundred years before the Declaration of Independence, Mohammedan government centered at Constantinople had better artillery than had we Christians in the West. The last effort they made to destroy Christendom failed during the last years of the seventeenth century, only just over two hundred years ago. Vienna was almost taken and only saved by the Christian army under the command of the King of Poland on a date that ought to be among the most famous in history: September 11, 1683.

November 4, 2001

WAR AND CIVILIZATION

After a lecture at a major New England university, a student asked a friend of mine who is a professor of philosophy, "When we speak of the Second World War, does that mean there was a first one?" Yes, it does. And the woeful neglect of history will be a deadly freight borne by the forming generation. Certainly one cannot be a Christian without a knowledge of history, since it is the result of history and explains history. Without roots in actual events, religion becomes a Gnostic vapor — that is, a sentimental illusion divorced from fact.

Veterans Day was first known as Armistice Day, because "the 11th hour of the 11th day of the 11th month" of 1918 was engraved in the memory of Western civilization. My maternal grandmother kept a framed poem in her house and bid me memorize it. She had two brothers in the Cheshire Regiment, formed in 1688, and both were killed within days of each other in 1915 in the Ypres Salient. A Canadian army surgeon, Lieutenant Colonel John McCrae, was aghast at what he saw on that battlefield, and within the space of about five minutes wrote the poem that became a template of the sadness that shrouded those fierce acres after seventeen days of battle:

> In Flanders fields the poppies blow
> Between the crosses row on row,
> That mark our place; and in the sky
> The larks, still bravely singing, fly
> Scarce heard amid the guns below.
> We are the Dead. Short days ago

We lived, felt dawn, saw sunset glow,
Loved and were loved, and now we lie
In Flanders fields.
Take up our quarrel with the foe:
To you from failing hands we throw
The torch; be yours to hold it high.
If ye break faith with us who die
We shall not sleep, though poppies grow
In Flanders fields.

Recently one of our parishioners returned from his second tour of duty in Iraq, grateful for the prayers of our people. We continue to pray for all those of our parish family engaged in this present war, in which the very norms of civilization are at stake. Even comfortable Europe is becoming more than anxious about threats to the culture it has taken for granted. In an essay of 1916, Theodore Roosevelt wrote:

> The Greeks who triumphed at Marathon and Salamis did a work without which the world would have been deprived of the social value of Plato and Aristotle, of Aeschylus, Herodotus, and Thucydides. The civilization of Europe, America, and Australia exists today at all only because of the victories of civilized man over the enemies of civilization, because the victories stretching through the centuries from the days of Miltiades and Themistocles to those of Charles Martel in the eighth century and those of John Sobieski in the seventeenth century.[30]

Now the challenge faces the twenty-first century.

November 5, 2006

---

[30] Theodore Roosevelt, "Social Values and National Existence," *Papers and Proceedings of the American Sociological Society* 9–10 (1916).

HE TODAY THAT SHEDS
HIS BLOOD WITH ME

The late Danish pianist and wit Victor Borge said that his father and uncle were identical twins, but he was not sure which was the identical one. Of St. Crispin and Crispinian, we know only that they were twins, possibly only fraternal. They preached the gospel to the Gauls, supporting themselves by working nights as shoemakers. Around the year 286, the governor Rictius Varus tried to drown them, and when that failed, they were beheaded. Shakespeare put their names on the lips of the twenty-nine-year-old King Henry V, rallying his outnumbered troops at Agincourt:

> This story shall the good man teach his son;
> And Crispin Crispian shall ne'er go by,
> From this day to the ending of the world,
> But we in it shall be remembered—
> We few, we happy few, we band of brothers;
> For he to-day that sheds his blood with me
> Shall be my brother; be he ne'er so vile,
> This day shall gentle his condition.

In life's daily spiritual battle, Christ promises to ennoble us as His brothers, once we offer our lives to Him. To initiate this process, He "emptied Himself, taking the form of a servant, being made in the likeness of men" (Phil. 2:7).

We speak with deceptive ease of the Word becoming flesh, but it was an astonishing condescension. In 1915 Franz Kafka published a story,

,"Die Verwandlung," or "The Metamorphosis," about a salesman who turns into an insect. His agony is that his words cannot be understood by those around him. The Incarnation of the Second Person of the Holy Trinity was more degrading than that, though the divine Love made it an act of beauty. Only love can understand the voice of the Incarnate Word: "His own people did not accept him, but to those who did accept Him, He gave power to become children of God" (John 1:11–12). In various expressions, the early Fathers taught what Clement of Alexandria said in a startling way: "The Logos of God became man so that you might learn from a man how a man may become God."[31] Lest this be misunderstood, Athanasius explains: "We are sons, not as the Son, as gods, not as He Himself." Our godliness is by grace, not nature: "not in essence but in sonship, which we shall partake from Him."

This month of All Saints celebrates holiness, not as a spectator sport, like fans cheering the holy souls from the bleachers and then saying, "We won!" Those who only observe from the sidelines the spiritual battles in which our culture is now engaged would be like those who were not at Agincourt.

> (They) shall think themselves accurs'd they were not here,
> And hold their manhoods cheap whiles any speaks
> That fought with us upon Saint Crispin's day.

November 6, 2011

---

31 Clement of Alexandria, *Exhortation to the Heathen*, chap. 1.

A FAMILY PARISH

Our parish is singularly blessed this Sunday in the octave of All Saints to dedicate the new sacred images in our sanctuary. Given the prominence of our parish's location in this world capital, I am grateful that these works of art have already attracted international interest. In times past, we may have underestimated the potential of our parish, and this public attention is one small step in recognizing that we are coming of age in proclaiming the Heavenly Kingdom.

The benefactions we have received from outside the parish to install these fine works of art are true gifts of God and free us to use our own money for the crucial work of restoring the roof and walls of this House of God. Such generosity should move us to examine our consciences: Are we this generous in terms of our own resources, whatever they may be, to promote the good works of our parish?

Some years ago, one of our parishioners brought to Mass a fine young son who, like many fine young sons, was a little rambunctious. She was informed by a matron that the Church of Our Saviour "is not a family parish." I am glad this got her Irish up and she stayed. Her fine young son is now a fine grown young man, and today we have more young people in the parish than ever before. We are also graced with many glorious senior people who have been faithful pillars of our parish for a long time. None should think that this parish's principal mission is entertaining ourselves. I am all for happy parties and hope that our approaching fiftieth-anniversary year will provide more of these, but we are redundant if our first purpose is not the preaching of the gospel and the salvation of souls.

The great image of Our Savior, blessed today, will preach in silence to those many who come here between the liturgies. The saints surrounding Him will remind us of our baptismal vocation to serve Christ as His soldiers until our life's end. Anything less than the best art we can provide is unworthy of Our Savior and too bourgeois for the beautiful building entrusted to us. For the Catholic, art is a necessity and not a luxury.

The youth of those artists and craftsmen who have worked on our new paintings is a bright hope for the future. They are recovering the classical traditions that the iconoclasts of the fading last generation scorned. One of our young artists was trained by his mother and grandmother, who studied art in their native China but were compelled to use their talents for propaganda art promoting cruel communism. Their gifted grandson and son[32] now lives in freedom and has painted not a dictator raising his fist but Christ Our Savior raising His hand in blessing over us.

November 7, 2004

---

[32] Father Rutler here refers to Ken Jan Woo, who in 2009 painted a much larger, internationally renowned, twenty-eight-foot-high image of *Christ Pantocrator* that, as of this writing, still dominates the sanctuary at the Church of Our Saviour—even after the priest who succeeded Father Rutler as pastor removed most of the other art and furnishings.

AHEAD OF THE TIMES

One assumes that the *New York Times* would have been glad to receive an op-ed article from the new archbishop of New York. The Archdiocese of New York is responsible for a very important part of the city's educational, medical, and charitable life. The newspaper refused to print it. But such censorship only whets the appetite to know what was thought not fit to print.

There are many items that the *Times*, which claims to publish everything that's fit to print, has printed, even though they were not fit. There were, for instance: its mockery in 1920 of Goddard's hypothesis that rocket propulsion can take place in a vacuum; a denial of Stalin's forced famine in Ukraine and a whitewash of his show trials by its Moscow bureau chief, Walter Duranty; its advocacy of Fidel Castro; and its benign regard for the Soviet spy Alger Hiss. Surely the paper must have suffered some journalistic equivalent of a cerebral stroke to render the editors of the *Times* unable to print Archbishop Dolan's words.

The cause of the apoplexy was the archbishop's imputation of bigotry to the newspaper. His charge was not self-indulgent whining. He did not have to go back further than a couple of weeks for examples. First, in reporting widespread child abuse in Brooklyn's community of Orthodox Jews, there was not the "selective outrage" that animates the *New York Times* against criminous Catholic clerics, whose numbers are in fact proportionally much smaller than other religious and professional groups.

Then there was the sensational front-page publicity of a paternity suit involving a Franciscan friar, going back twenty-five years, and getting more space than the war in Afghanistan and genocide in Sudan.

Headlines also claimed that the Pope was seeking to "lure" Anglicans into his fold, when in fact he was responding to a petition. Then a columnist invoked the Inquisition, portrayed the theology of priesthood as neurotic sexism, and even mocked the Pope's haberdashery. The archbishop said that the paper's prejudice, "while maybe appropriate for the Know-Nothing newspaper of the 1850's, *The Menace*, has no place in a major publication today." While a free press is free to criticize, said the archbishop, such criticism should be "fair, rational, and accurate."[33]

Hostility raised to such a pitch that journalistic standards are abandoned is perhaps provoked by an awareness that the Catholic Church continues to be the substantial voice for classical moral standards and supernatural confidence amid the noise of a disintegrating, behaviorist culture. A tabloid is still a tabloid, even if its editors dress in tweeds. Churchill said, "No folly is more costly than the folly of intolerant idealism." Not to worry. Christ promised that the gates of Hell will not prevail against His Church. He did not include the *New York Times*, 30 percent of whose work force has been laid off in the last year and a half.[34]

November 8, 2009

---

[33] "*New York Times* Refuses to Publish Archbishop Dolan's Op-Ed on Anti-Catholic Bias," Catholic News Agency, October 30, 2009, http://www.catholicnewsagency.com/.

[34] The *Times*'s financial slide has continued. Net profit last year was down 60 percent.

THE BLOOD OF HER BISHOPS

An astute professor once said that political wrangling in universities is so vicious because the stakes are so small. There are those in proverbial ivory towers who will struggle to get control of a faculty or become an assistant dean with an animus that would ill befit a general in battle. There is one caveat, though: the stakes are not so small when you consider that professors can shape the minds of a whole generation.

A recent letter in the *New York Times* signed by progressive Catholic academics objected that a columnist had no right to comment on the recent synod in Rome[35] because he had no theology degree. It seemed to ignore the fact that none of that newspaper's columnists who frequently attack Catholic doctrine have any such scholarly decorations. The petitioners' quibble over credentials also seemed to defy the progressives' stand for more vocal involvement of the laity.

Academia is rife with censorship in the form of political correctness, but it cannot totally smother the truth, which is supposed to be the substance and goal of learning, expressed in the plethora of school mottoes: Veritas, Lux et Veritas, Veritas Vos Liberabit, and so on.

---

[35] In 2015, the Synod on the Family fanned hope in dissenting religious and academics that Christ's teaching on the permanence of marriage might be overturned. Liberal German bishops pushed to allow Catholics who had divorced and remarried outside the Church to receive Holy Communion. In the synod's summary, they managed to include a suggestion that a local bishop, rather than a Vatican tribunal, might judge such situations "case by case" in the light of "mercy"—free to improvise Church teaching on mortal sin, the laws of marriage, and Christ's Real Presence in the Eucharist.

An example of insuppressible prophecy was Dr. Anca-Maria Cernea, a representative of the Association of Catholic Doctors of Bucharest, Romania, at the Synod on the Family in Rome. In the midst of speeches of varying quality, her brief remarks set a unique tone in the assembly of bishops and consultants. She spoke of her parents, who were engaged to be married, but waited seventeen years while her father was a political prisoner of her country's communist dictatorship. Her mother kept vigil all that time, not knowing whether he was dead or alive.

Dr. Cernea went on to say:

> The Church's mission is to save souls. Evil, in this world, comes from sin. Not from income disparity or "climate change." The solution is: Evangelization. Conversion. Not an ever-increasing government control. Not a world government. These are nowadays the main agents imposing cultural Marxism on our nations.... Our Church was suppressed by the Soviet occupation. But none of our 12 bishops betrayed their communion with the Holy Father.... Now we need Rome to tell the world: "Repent of your sins and turn to God, for the Kingdom of Heaven is near."[36]

Seven of the twelve bishops she mentioned died in prison. It was a sobering reflection during a synod where there were not a few receptions and much dining—pleasures innocent in themselves, but different in tone from the laments of the countless Christians suffering in the Middle East. It was also very different in urgency from the offended academics whose pomposity was pricked by an "unqualified" newspaper columnist. They would have been more offended by the Romanian doctor whose only theological credentials were bestowed by the witness of her parents and the blood of her bishops.

November 8, 2015

---

[36] Dr. Cernea Speech to Synod, *Catholic Medical Quarterly* 66, no. 1 (February 2016), http://www.cmq.org.uk/.

The Poison of False Wisdom

It is a Roman custom for students in the pontifical universities to attend Mass in St. Peter's Basilica at the opening of the academic year. On October 30, Pope Benedict XVI told the students and professors that when St. Paul exhorted Christians to "become fools" in the eyes of the world, he was not being anti-intellectual. St. Paul did not mind boasting of his own academic laurels when he had to, but he did it ironically to explain the limits of human intelligence, warning against "a way of living and seeing things divorced from God, following dominant opinions according to the criteria of success and power." The Pope called pride "the poison of false wisdom."[37]

The gift of faith and the virtue of humility save us from false wisdom. I am writing early in the week, before our nation chooses whether its future course will be fatal or providential. Suffice it to say that the lack of faith and humility always lends credence to false wisdom and bogus prophets. Christ is the One and none other. Neglect of sound teaching by many in the Church created a generation of people naïvely ignorant of the basic precepts of the Church and bereft of logic in ordering their thought. They even claim that the definition of life itself is "above my pay grade."[38] The great challenge of our time now is to repair this.

---

[37] "Holy Father Denounces Pride, Teaches Way to True Wisdom," Catholic News Agency, October 31, 2008, http://www.catholicnewsagency.com/.

[38] As a presidential candidate, Barack Obama was described as brilliant, knowledgeable, and borderline messianic by Democratic operatives, the national media, and his own campaign literature. Yet when liberal pastor Rick Warren publicly asked him his position on when a human life

A brother priest of mine in New England recently reminded his flock that to be "orthodox" means "not being conservative or liberal, but being in union of 'mind and heart,' as we say in the Eucharistic prayer, with the Pope, our Bishop, and the Faith of the Church—the whole Faith, not just those parts we find palatable or acceptable." He adds:

> Now let us be very clear: You can be heterodox and be a fine, loving, caring person—perhaps more loving, caring and all-round cuddly than many an orthodox person—that is not the point. The point is, as held true for centuries in the Church, do you accept unequivocally what the Church holds and teaches as dogma and doctrine? Do you give assent of mind and heart to what Holy Mother the Church states must be believed? If you do, you are neither liberal nor conservative, you are orthodox; if you do not, you are heterodox. The concept of "dissent" from Church teaching—and even dialogue with dissent—would have been unheard of in the life of the early Church. The reason people today rush to the use of aggressive political labels to describe a person's practice or defense of the Faith is because personal opinion is now regarded as the litmus test of truth.

The Holy Father encourages all of us to "dedicate ourselves to intellectual work, free of the temptation of pride, and boast always and only in the Lord."[39]

November 9, 2008

---

begins, he had no answer—or perhaps didn't want to say. As a junior senator from Illinois, he had voted against the Born-Alive Infants Protection Act—which outlawed partial-birth abortion.

Obama's answer to the pastor's question was, "That's above my pay grade." And yet, in 2013, in his final presidential term, Obama had the distinction of being the first sitting U.S. president not only to speak at a Planned Parenthood function but publicly to say, "Thank you, Planned Parenthood. God bless you."

[39] "Holy Father Denounces Pride."

A Parish Is Not an Heirloom, but a Military Base

The proposed realignment of parishes is complete for now. The most recent segment of the process called "Making All Things New" was extensive and even draconian, and representatives of our parish participated in it faithfully and patiently. Their work has borne good fruit. Contrary to some recommendations, both churches for which I am responsible, St. Michael's and Holy Innocents, will remain open.

A parish is a "juridical person" that cannot close, but may be merged. Holy Innocents remains as is for the foreseeable future. St. Michael's is in the unique position of being amidst the most extensive development of commercial and residential properties in the history of our nation. Along with the astronomical rise in the value of the area's real estate are the increasing numbers of residents and commuters, with improved access to public transportation via a new subway stop that is to open nearby. These are considerable matters in configuring the future of our Catholic witness.

The Church of St. Michael was established in 1857 near the current site of the Pennsylvania Station and was moved to our present location fifty years later, preserving much of the church's art and stonework. Our present situation is being "monitored" to determine if another relocation into the heart of the Hudson Yards development will be prudent some years from now. While there may be nostalgic connections to buildings, nostalgia is not holy tradition, for the latter is the dynamic transmission of unchanging Faith.

In any battle, sometimes a battalion holds its ground, and sometimes it makes a strategic move. How that works for us has yet to be determined. A parish is not a family heirloom, but a military base. We are engaged in a spiritual battle in our culture, greater than any physical struggle, for we are engaged against "principalities and powers" not of this world. It is not an exaggeration to say that the fate of the city depends far less on improved schools and transportation and health and social welfare than it does on bringing the life of Christ to a culture that is spiritually traumatized.

The number of people in New York City who currently identify themselves as Catholic is about the same as it was seventy years ago. Yet back then, weekly Mass attendance in the city was over 70 percent, and now it is about 12 percent. Most of the decline occurred in the conflicted time immediately following the Second Vatican Council. In recent years, the decline in attendance has leveled off, but the numbers have yet to increase. If all Catholics were serious about their response to Christ's call, there would be no redundant churches.

The first stage in spiritual health is to have a good examination of conscience, just like a physical examination. When the doctor says your body mass has to be improved, you trim down, exercise, and eat well. Spiritual fitness is the same: we need to slim down what drags us down, worship, and be nurtured by the sacraments. Then comes the new strength.

November 9, 2014

WHO AM I? ONLY GOD CAN
TELL US THE ANSWER

The wistfulness of these autumnal days moves the mind, by the natural withering of leaves and the shortening of days, to think of the end of our own lives. The brilliant burst of colors in these darkening days is nature's signature that there is something bright about the death of things. The Church designates November for serious thought about the mystery of mortality and eternal life. Without this, we would be like aimless people with vacant eyes wondering who and why we are.

That was the reason classical philosophers strove to examine their thoughts and behavior, believing the maxim that the unexamined life is not worth living. Inscribed in the forecourt of the temple of Apollo at Delphi were the words *gnothi seauton*: "Know yourself." Even before that, in the temple of Luxor in Egypt, was written, "Know yourself ... and you shall know the gods."

We could be very basic and literal and take that to mean knowledge about our bodies, and, in fact, in the sixteenth century, the Latin version — *Nosce te ipsum* — was written on the front of anatomical atlases showing dissected bodies. That is not how the great philosophers meant it, and everyone admits that you can have a detailed knowledge of your bones and brains and kidneys, and still not know who you are. "What am I?" needs to be "Who am I?" — and only God can answer that.

This is why the book of Revelation says: "To the one who is victorious, I will give some of the hidden manna. I will also give him a white stone with a new name written on it, known only to the one who receives it"

(2:17). As with the deepest mysteries revealed by God, there is room in this present world for conjecture. The meaning of that white stone has elicited various theories. Juries in ancient Greece would cast a white stone if they found the defendant innocent. But there was no name on it. Fast forward a little, and the Romans gave tesserae, which were small stones, as a sort of ticket of admission to public events, but they were not necessarily white. Since this passage in Revelation has Christ speaking to the church in Pergamum, it could be a reference to that city's temple of Asclepius, on whose pillars people who had been healed wrote their names, rather as is done now in Lourdes and Fatima.

Perhaps the simplest and best explanation is that the Romans of old awarded white stones to winners of the athletic games as tokens for admission to the victory banquet. All we need to know in these fading days of the year is that the eternal Christ invites us each day of our lives to live as though we were dying, so that in dying we might live forever.

November 10, 2013

CELEBRITIES AND SAINTS

With the exception of puppies in pet-shop windows, nothing stops traffic like celebrities. Most celebrity fades as fickle taste moves on. Around A.D. 66, when St. Jude was writing his letter and St. Paul was being beheaded, the Greek historian Plutarch wrote his *Parallel Lives* comparing famous Greeks with Roman celebrities. Few of us today would recognize most of the stars he wrote about: Agesilaus, Pelopidas, Philopoemen, Sertorius, Aemilius Paulus, and so on. The crowds that flocked to see Flaminius and Poplicola would have passed St. Peter and St. Paul on the street with nary a glance. None of them had the slightest idea who Jesus was, but everyone knew Lucullus and Sulla.

The Nobel Peace Prize was awarded to Emily Balch, Fridtjof Nansen and Bertha von Suttner, but I doubt Oprah Winfrey would recognize any of them. Last Sunday the Holy Father beatified Juan Nepomuceno Zegri y Moreno of Granada (1831–1905), Bonifacia Rodriguez Castro of Salamanca (1837–1905), Valentin Paquay of Belgium (1828–1905), Luigi Maria Monti of Italy (1825–1900), and Rosalie Rendu of France (1786–1856). Even most Catholics know less about them than they do about some of the names in the gossip columns of our city's tabloids.

The saints have the advantage of a celebrity given by God and not by men, and so they do not fade like film "stars." I recently was astonished that not half a dozen of our bright young parishioners had ever heard of Greer Garson, who in the early 1940s was "one of the most famous women in the world." On the other hand, I knew little about some of the Hollywood actors who were in our parish this past week making a film for Paramount Pictures. I admit that I knew more about some of

Plutarch's celebrities than about the very pleasant Meryl Streep and Denzel Washington. May they prosper.

Celebrities can use their fame to promote much good. But people can be disappointed in falling stars. "Say it ain't so, Joe," ran the headline in the *Chicago Daily News* when White Sox star Shoeless Joe Jackson was accused in a 1919 game-throwing scandal. A few people committed suicide when Rudolph Valentino was buried from St. Malachy's Church, but they've stopped doing that now.

All alone in his last exile, Napoleon was amazed that after eighteen hundred years, Jesus still had people dying for Him. The fame of Jesus was not given to him. Jesus sheds His light on others: "You have not chosen me. I have chosen you" (John 15:16). The only lasting stars are those who have their radiance from "the Father of Lights" (James 1:17). The calendar of saints is the charter of the one reliable fan club. So in this month of the saints and holy souls, the Church sings:

> Who are these, like stars appearing,
> These before God's throne who stand?
> Each a golden crown is wearing;
> Who are all this glorious band?
> Alleluia, hark! They sing,
> Praising loud their heavenly King.

November 11, 2003

SMASHING THE ICONS OF CIVILIZATION

In London, the Kensington and Chelsea Council is considering plans to erect a new statue of Our Lady of Walsingham at Chelsea Embankment Gardens on the site of the former home of St. Thomas More. When the saint was executed by Henry VIII, his home was given to the king's chief minister and agent for the destruction of the monasteries and other Catholic properties, Thomas Cromwell—who removed the old statue of Our Lady of Walsingham from its famous Norfolk shrine and publicly burned it on the grounds of More's former residence. He burned other statues, including the Black Madonna of Willesden, one of whose devotees was the king's own mother, Elizabeth of York. It is hoped that the new statue, which will include a memorial of the ransacked monasteries, will be dedicated on June 22, the feast of St. Thomas More. The executive director of the Kensington and Chelsea Council said that it will "mark both the artistic vandalism and religious intolerance" of that period.

Those dark days were not unique. Another Cromwell—Oliver— along with such as Calvin, Robespierre, Stalin, and Ceausescu do not have high places in the history of art and were to Catholicism what the Taliban were to Buddhism. Our generation has passed through another wave of iconoclasm from which the Church is just starting to recover. This iconoclasm, unlike previous movements, was self-inflicted by misguided liturgists and compliant authorities in the name of the Second Vatican Council, which, as Pope Benedict has reminded us, never intended such demolition.

Recently, one of the most beautiful churches in our own archdiocese was saved from such renovation by the happy intervention of our cardinal, but over the years many other churches were not so fortunate. Most of our parish's treasures are preserved, and our beautiful altar rail was never removed. Some years ago I found candlesticks in our basement that had been specially designed for the church. Blackened and in disrepair, they were restored and now shine on the high altar. In adjusted inflation dollars, the six large ones cost $36,000 and the eight smaller ones for the side altars cost $24,000. Four of them have been recovered. The original tabernacle, crafted at a cost of $90,000, was demolished, but in recent years it has been replaced. Some years ago, the baptismal font, of rare marble at a cost of $30,000 was removed to the garden and is beyond repair, but we have been able to restore the baptistery, including long-hidden carved cabinetry, and were blessed to secure a magnificent font from the closed St. Ann's Church, which is even finer than our original.

There seems to be a resurgence of excellent architects and artists, quite of few of whom belong to our own parish. It may be that a "New Springtime" of the Church's heritage is about to appear, but after a long winter.

November 11, 2007

HURRICANES, THE DARK, AND THE LIGHT

During the days following Hurricane Sandy, we had no electric light in our church for five days, and as I am writing this in time for the printer, we still have no heat, and my fingers are pretty cold as they type on a cold keyboard. We can be thankful for the many ways our parishioners have been helping out in these days, and we are not unaware of the needs of those who worship here, who have gone through sore trials: evacuated from our local hospitals; homes burned to the ground; and at least one whose house was washed out into the ocean. For many days, we relied on candlepower for Masses and confessions. I read from the Missal on the altar with the help of a candlestick that had belonged to a great-great-grandfather who was in the Crimean War. While the electricity failed, the candlestick still served its purpose. My ancestor could not have imagined that one day it would be used for Mass in America, but it was for me a nostalgic moment.

Now, nostalgia has been called "history after a few drinks": we remember the best and filter out the worst. Nostalgia lacks the vitality of tradition, which Chesterton called "the democracy of the dead." Tradition means passing something on, and Sacred Tradition passes on what is holy. Tradition is lively and life-giving, uniting past, present, and future in a spiritual continuum, as Christ was and is and will be.

Like the old candlestick that sheds light when electric power fails, the light of Christ does not go out. The same voice that said, "Let there be light" billions of years ago, sheds light on us today. And "the darkness had not overcome it" (John 1:5). Certainly there are those who choose the darkness of evil to the light of goodness: "For everyone who does wicked things hates the light and does not come toward the light, so that his works might not be exposed. But whoever lives the truth comes to the light, so that his works may be clearly seen as done in God" (John 3:20–21).

Those who oppose Christ have their day, but it does not last long, and soon they also have their night, when they shrink away into dark corners. In the great challenge of our culture, we are free to choose light or darkness. God is pro-choice: He has given us a free will. But He is only pro-*right*-choice. The exercise of choice is not self-justifying. Only the choice of the light of Christ can save us from the darkness of Satan. And what better authority can we have for this than our holy God Himself? "I have set before you life and death, the blessing and the curse. Choose life, then, that you and your descendants may live" (Deut. 30:19).

November 11, 2012

A Church Building, and
the Echo of the Cold War

In this year celebrating the golden anniversary of the dedication of our church, it is fitting that we should be burnishing its gilt and gold. The original expense of the building precluded completing all that was decoratively envisioned. New generations add their own gifts.

Our side shrines are being finished in the style of their period by skilled volunteers. Since August, more than one hundred man-hours of work have gone into this project, as well as work on the Shrine of Our Lady and the Baptistry.

The iconography in the sanctuary is now completed with figures of Moses and Elijah and two angels worshipping our Savior. Ken Jan Woo devoted four months to "writing" these images, which are based on the Transfiguration icon of Theophanes the Greek (ca. 1330–ca. 1410) for a church in Novgorod. Theophanes was a colleague and tutor of Andrei Rublev (1370–1430). The Novgorod icon, which now is in the Tretyakov Gallery of Moscow, suits the transitional Romanesque architecture of our church and is one of the images particularly admired by Pope Benedict XVI. The angels are of the Sienese school, also representative of the Italian transition from medieval to Renaissance art, like our church itself. Using our local talent, we have been able to glorify God's House at practically no cost, while budgeting more than we ever have for the church's charitable works.

Our church was dedicated at the most intense time of the Cold War. Parishioners then would have been gratified that those involved in these recent installations are young people who survived communism. Ken Woo's family endured the Chinese Cultural Revolution, and families of the workers who braved high scaffolding for these installations lived in Poland in its last years of Marxist control.

I am writing on the twentieth anniversary of the fall of the Berlin Wall. We in the West, with no experience of the Church's heroic suffering, may be tempted to take freedom for granted and to be seduced by contemporary dilettantes who disdain Christian culture and even praise figures like Mao and his heirs.

The political philosopher Leszek Kolakowski died this summer in Oxford. His father had been killed by the Gestapo during the German occupation of Poland, and he secretly taught himself to read. Having hoped Marxism would change things, he eventually saw through it and was expunged from the party. He wrote: "Communism was not the crazy fantasy of a few fanatics, nor the result of human stupidity and baseness; it was a real, very real part of the history of the twentieth century, and we cannot understand this history of ours without understanding communism. We cannot get rid of this specter by saying it was just 'human stupidity,' or 'human corruptibility.' The specter is stronger than the spells we cast on it. It might come back to life."

November 15, 2009

Happiness and Holiness

Since Arturo Toscanini lived to be nearly ninety, dying in the Bronx, I was able as a boy to watch an orchestra conducted by this man—who had led the premiere of *Pagliacci* in 1892. In operas like that and *Otello*, divas never get a better chance to hit a high E-flat than when they are being strangled or stabbed.

It is said that Pope Benedict XV's last words in 1922 were the same as in Leoncavallos's opera after Nedda and her lover, Silvio, are slain: *"La commedia è finita!"* Lest one think that the Pope's domestic life was unruly, the line was first used at the end of Haydn's more decorous opera *Il Mondo della Luna*. Anti-Catholic polemicists, whose less-than-rudimentary Italian imputes cynicism to the Pope, infer from this that his reign and the papacy itself were a farce. If the Pope's words were as claimed, he spoke of *commedia* as did Dante: the drama of the Pope's life was ending, and he had fulfilled the work assigned him. It was a happy ending, though the world around him had passed through a terrible sadness of war.

Aristotle's concept of happiness as the goal of life is different from run-of-the-mill notions of happiness defined as feeling satisfied. His *eudaemonia* is the serenity that comes from a virtuous life lived with balance and dignity.

There are different kinds of laughter. Professor Ronald Berk (biostatistician emeritus of Johns Hopkins University), has categorized them: snicker, giggle, chuckle, chortle, laugh, cackle, guffaw, howl, shriek, roar, and convulsion. You can see how they gradually degenerate from Aristotelian serenity. One must be suspicious of the media cynosure, rampant in politics and such, who laughs habitually, with the same pose and bluster.

I do not mean the madman who laughs at what is not funny, but the calculator who laughs for effect: sometimes out of insecurity and often to ingratiate and manipulate, a clown outside and a cad inside. It is the sardonic impulse of one who does not want the people on deck to see the looming iceberg, or who cajoles you into buying the Brooklyn Bridge.

The Lady of Lourdes told St. Bernadette: "I promise you happiness — not in this world, but in the other." The Lady did not laugh, but bestowed on Bernadette a smile that she keeps today in realms above. And the Lady's Son is not recorded as guffawing (although His amiable fraternity was like none other), but He came that our joy might be full. "These things I have spoken to you, that in me you may have peace. In the world you shall have distress; but have confidence, I have overcome the world" (John 16:33).

November 15, 2015

PREPARED FOR SPIRITUAL COMBAT

In February of 1943, the ill-prepared United States Army II Corps valiantly fought against the German-Italian Panzer Army at the Kasserine Pass in Tunisia, but had to retreat. The army did wake up, commanders were replaced, the troops regrouped, and eventually the war was won. This is a contemporary allegory, when we see the social consequences of poorly formed Catholics overwhelmed by secular forces that have no love for the Church.

In the nineteenth century, Cardinal Newman warned that naïve Catholics would fall into "mass apostasy" through lack of preparedness in spiritual combat:

> Do you think (the Prince of Lies) is so unskillful in his craft, as to ask you openly and plainly to join him in his warfare against the Truth? No; he offers you baits to tempt you. He promises you civil liberty; he promises you equality; he promises you trade and wealth; he promises you a remission of taxes; he promises you reform. This is the way in which he conceals from you the kind of work to which he is putting you; he tempts you to rail against your rulers and superiors; he does so himself, and induces you to imitate him; or he promises you illumination — he offers you knowledge, science, philosophy, enlargement of mind.
>
> He scoffs at times gone by; he scoffs at every institution which reveres them. He prompts you what to say, and then listens to you, and praises you, and encourages you. He bids you mount aloft. He shows you how to become as gods. Then he laughs and jokes with

you, and gets intimate with you; he takes your hand, and gets his fingers between yours, and grasps them, and then you are his.[40]

Many have warned about the consequences of yielding the Faith to false messiahs. Years before becoming Pope, Benedict XVI wrote: "Wherever politics tries to be redemptive, it is promising too much. Where it wishes to do the work of God, it becomes not divine, but demonic."[41]

We are about to witness many outrages against the dignity of life by politicians who have taken advantage of nominal Christians.[42] For starters, we may expect removal of the present administration's ban on destructive embryonic research, and rejection of the Mexico City accords that restrained abortion and eugenics. Most immediately, the New York State legislature has proposed a bill removing the statute of limitations on lawsuits that would damage, and possibly bankrupt, Catholic and other private institutions. Since Cardinal Egan wrote his letter about this, the recent election gave both houses of the legislature to the party that favors this bill.

As with the lesson of the Kasserine Pass, we are learning that there is no place for amateur soldiers in the army of the Lord. A short time from now, many will say: "We should have listened to the warnings."

The hard response will be: "Why didn't you?"

November 16, 2008

---

[40] John Henry Newman, Tract 83, June 29, 1838.
[41] Benedict XVI, *Truth and Tolerance* (San Francisco: Ignatius Press, 2005), 116.
[42] Father Rutler proved correct in these predictions—made in the aftermath of the election of Barack Obama.

Where Earth and Heaven Meet

The feast of the Dedication of the Basilica of St. John Lateran last week was a twofold reminder of the importance of that church, which is the Pope's cathedral and, like all churches, an expression of the unity found in communion with the successor of St. Peter. It is also an important sign that all church buildings are expressions of Heaven.

In Jerusalem, Our Lord said that if the Temple were destroyed, He would rebuild it in three days. He was speaking of His own body, for buildings come and go, but He lives forever. Yet He revered the earthly Temple and became most righteously angry, using a whip to drive out those who profaned it. Each one of us by baptism becomes a temple of the Holy Spirit, and the best way to keep that human shrine fit for God is to whip Satan out of it by going to confession.

Church buildings are natural lodgings for the supernatural Church, which is why we should make them as beautiful as possible. Winston Churchill said, "We shape our buildings, and afterwards our buildings shape us."

The art and skill with which we adorn churches in turn bring us closer to the Lord. It is not enough to believe in Christ. The acknowledgment of His divinity must move the soul to worship Him. "The devils also believe and tremble in fear" (James 2:19), because they refuse to worship him. Their fear is servile fear, and not the holy fear, or awe, that churches should evoke and encourage. It is the difference between being haunted and being holy.

Jesus called the Temple "My Father's house" because He is the Divine Son. We pray "Our Father" and not "My Father" because we are not divine by nature, but God "adopts" us as His children, and so church buildings express in stone what we are in flesh. They should not be like lecture halls or living rooms, but should be places where earth and Heaven meet. To enter a church is to confess that our relationship with God is a corporate obedience to His will and not an individualistic exercise of arbitrary opinions.

Hundreds of churches have been destroyed recently in Iraq and Syria. Christians there paradoxically become ever more vividly Christian by their terrible suffering. When we get into a lather about merging churches in our city, and act as though the closing of a church building were the end of the world, we should rather ask ourselves if we could be servants of God without a particular building of which we have become fond. In all things, including church architecture, faith offers God the best we can give. But without the devotion of the heart, asceticism fades away into vain aestheticism. A wise liturgist once said that the best way to make a church beautiful is to fill it with people.

November 16, 2014

The One Who Stands Firm to the End

This past November 9 and 10 marked the seventy-fifth anniversary of *Kristallnacht*, when mobs attacked properties belonging to Jews in Berlin and other German cities. Synagogues, hospitals, and schools were defaced or destroyed, 91 were killed, and 30,000 Jews were sent to prototypical concentration camps. It was a bold declaration of the Nazi intent to destroy a people. Many Germans nobly acted with revulsion at what had become of their government. One man symbolic of such was Cardinal Michael von Faulhaber, archbishop of Munich, who helped the Chief Rabbi of the city rescue the Torah and sacred vessels before his synagogue was attacked. The Nazis ransacked the cardinal's home and threatened him with Dachau. He survived all that, and in 1951 he ordained two young brothers, one of whom would become Pope Benedict XVI.

This is not just a historical vignette, for tragic events often repeat themselves in different forms and circumstances when people ignore them, and much of the world in 1938 tried to treat *Kristallnacht* as an isolated incident with no portent of worse things to come. The sad fact is that our days are witnessing widespread hostility to Jews and Christians alike in many places, and much of the media turns its attention away. This is sometimes because there is an aversion to offending the persecutors, some of whom are assisted by U.S. tax money in the form of foreign aid and military assistance. Sometimes there is just a bias against Judeo-Christian culture on the part of secularists who are glad to see the followers of Western religion bleed — and fail to conclude that Western atheists might be next. Indeed, some Western sophisticates cast a blind eye to Nazism in the 1930s because the National Socialists explained themselves as enemies of Marxism.

The revival of anti-Semitism in Europe today is accompanied by hostility to Christianity, and this is not limited to Europe. Many of our own public institutions deny freedom of speech to Christians, and public professions of faith in Christ receive a hostile reception in significant parts of academe. Christianity is evaporating in the Middle East as Christians are leaving countries where roots go back to the earliest apostolic foundations. The beheading of converts to Christianity hardly seems exceptional anymore. In Iran, Kazakh Christians are intimidated by the arrest of their pastors, and churches are destroyed from Egypt to Pakistan. The recent massacre of Christians in a Kenyan shopping mall could not be overlooked by the secular press, but it was soon forgotten, and there is little outrage at the imprisonment and torture of thousands of Christians in Eritrean desert camps. Countless Christians are being persecuted in *odium fidei*—"hatred of the Faith." Their bravery should humble us who live in calmer places, but it is also a warning that echoes Christ Himself: "Everyone will hate you because of me, but the one who stands firm to the end will be saved" (Mark 13:13).

November 17, 2013

Thanksgiving — the Beginning
of Holiness

Thanksgiving Day is rather late in the year for a harvest festival. The fields have been harvested many weeks past, which is why most countries have their festivals in October. We urban dwellers are a bit fuzzy about these things. The closest we get to amber waves of grain may be Gristedes. Frozen foods and air transport mean that we can eat any kind of vegetable any time of year, and Chilean sea bass is not exotic in Manhattan anymore. Thanksgiving Day attests that the earth's bounty is not to be taken for granted, and that we have been especially blessed in our nation with a freedom from want that is unique in history.

This day is one time when the Church obliges the bidding of the civil government for prayer. It is not a holy day of obligation, for such holy days celebrate aspects of the mystery of redemption. The president asks all citizens to give thanks to God for all of our nation's blessings, the first of which is the bread by which we live.

It is ironic that the Puritan settlers in the Plymouth Colony are so much associated with a thanksgiving feast, because they were dogmatically opposed to ritual feasts, and they had rejected the Holy Eucharist, which supernatural grace makes into the highest possible act of thanksgiving. We have been told often enough that *eucharist* is "thanksgiving" in Greek.

Thanksgiving is almost a definition of civility, Puritan or Catholic. Parents begin to civilize their little ones when they get a gift: "What do you say?" And the answer "thank you" starts the child on the paths of all good things. This is more than a lesson in etiquette. It is training in the art of an eternal grace: saying thanks to the giver changes a passive receiver into an active associate of some sort. That is not putting it well, but it does help to explain how gracious thanksgiving can make people into good citizens, earthly and heavenly, by making them patriots and saints. The categories are not inseparable, but neither are they contradictory.

A nation that ignores its God loses its soul, the way any individual does. In time of war, a day of thanksgiving remembers the harvest fields, but also the battlefields,[43] praying for the victory of justice, and thanking God for a civilization that we took too often for granted without saying "thank you," until it was attacked before our very eyes.

November 18, 2001

---

[43] This column was written in anticipation of the first Thanksgiving after 9/11.

PROPHETS WITHOUT HONOR

Our Lord predicted that "the sun will be darkened, and the moon will not give its light" (Mark 13:24). In every generation, there will be efforts to block Christ (the sun) and muffle the voice of His Church (the moon).

Cardinal Consalvi reminded Napoleon that even weak bishops for nineteen centuries had not been able to block the voice of Christ. A century and a half later, when his Vichy government claimed Catholic credentials but promoted genocide, Pierre Laval blustered, "Nobody and nothing can sway me from my determination to rid France of foreign Jews. Cardinals and bishops have intervened, but everyone is a master of his own trade. They handle religion. I handle government." Three years later, Laval was executed, and in 1981 a chief object of Laval's threats, Cardinal Gerlier, was posthumously declared "Righteous among the Nations" by Yad Vashem.

In 1980, Cardinal Medeiros of Boston wrote: "Those who make abortion possible by law cannot separate themselves from the guilt which accompanies this horrendous crime and deadly sin." Shortly afterward, the cardinal visited my college in Rome. He recounted how Senator Edward Kennedy told him: "You do your business, and I'll do mine." The next year, Cardinal Madieros died unexpectedly in heart surgery at the age of sixty-seven.

On November 12, the bishop of Providence, Thomas J. Tobin, responded to a public comment of Congressman Patrick Kennedy, who had said: "The fact that I disagree with the hierarchy on some issues does not make me any less of a Catholic." The bishop asked, "What does it mean to be a Catholic?" and then quoted the Congregation for the Doctrine of the Faith: "It would be a mistake to confuse the proper autonomy exercised by Catholics in political life with the claim of a principle that prescinds from the moral and social teaching of the Church." The bishop gave a checklist for being a Catholic that applies to each of us:

> Do you accept the teachings of the Church on essential matters of faith and morals, including our stance on abortion? Do you belong to a local Catholic community, a parish? Do you attend Mass on Sundays and receive the sacraments regularly? Do you support the Church personally, publicly, spiritually and financially?

In 1947 Cardinal Ritter of St. Louis threatened to excommunicate any of his flock who tried to stop the racial integration of Catholic schools, and in 1962 Archbishop Rummel of New Orleans did in fact excommunicate a judge and two other Catholics for opposing desegregation. The media hailed them as prophets. But when newer bishops in the mold of Benedict XVI refuse to play courtier to decadent dynasties, voices older than Laval, and as old as Pilate, whine with a tone of lèse-majesté: "Mind your own business."

November 22, 2009

THE END OF THE BEGINNING

On September 27, 1959, His Eminence Francis Cardinal Spellman solemnly blessed the Church of Our Saviour. The parish had been chartered on September 30, 1955, and the first Sunday Mass was celebrated in the Midston House, which stood on the site of the present Doral Hotel. Daily services began on Ash Wednesday in 1956 in a provisional chapel at 72 Park Avenue. Auxiliary Bishop Joseph Donahue broke ground for the church on April 1 of the same year, and on Christmas Eve, 1957, the Blessed Sacrament was transferred from the little chapel to the completed undercroft of the new church, where the first Mass was celebrated on Christmas Day. Construction continued on the rest of the building, and the upper church was first used on Ash Wednesday in 1959.

An aluminum company offered to donate the complete structural frame of the church, provided that the design be in the latest modernistic style of the 1950s. This was not done, and that nadir of architecture did not inflict an eyesore on Park Avenue. Because no expense seemed to be spared, we have what we now have: all the bronze work, woodcarvings, and inlays are treasures. Modern engineering enhanced Romanesque design, and the newspapers marveled at the skill used to place the two Languedoc marble columns in the sanctuary, six tons each, which, after being quarried in France, were polished in Italy and remain the largest uncut marble columns in the city. Factors including the immense expense of construction made payment of the mortgage debt a long process. Some thought it would never be paid, and many even said Cardinal Spellman had made a mistake.

The *Code of Canon Law* as it then obtained did not allow for the con-secration of a church in debt. One could not give to God what was owned by a bank. The church was dedicated and the altars consecrated, with relics, but the full consecration, with anointing of the walls, would await the payment of the mortgage. The Solemn Dedication of the church on December 9 will complete the rituals begun in 1959.

As we look forward to Thanksgiving Day, we add gratitude that this dedication also approaches. Like a graduation or an ordination, it is in truth the completion of a preparation. The work of caring for what we have inherited and growing in Christian witness now enters a new phase. Some of our original parishioners are still with us, and deserve to enjoy these moments. Many new parishioners and friends will want to do their part.

We can be Churchillian about this spiritual challenge by saying that it is not the end, it is not even the beginning of the end, but it is the end of the beginning.

November 24, 2002

NO STATE CAN REWRITE REALITY

The Solemnity of Our Lord Jesus Christ, King of the Universe, is a modern celebration. Pope Pius XI added it to the liturgical calendar in 1925, inspired to contradict the growing statism of communist and fascist movements that would give the civil authority preeminence over all human affairs.

Eight decades ago, in Germany, Bishop Johannes Schmidt preached on the feast of Christ the King against the neo-pagan attempt of the National Socialists to replace the spiritual realm of the Church with a new social order based on racism and national interests. The Vatican Radio broadcast his "magnificent sermon" to Germany in German, including his comment that no state has a right to rewrite reality: "Twice two makes four, whether you are a Japanese, a German or an Eskimo. There is a truth common to all mankind, and every nation is but a different incarnation of the same truth about man."

There are influences in our culture today that want Christ to abdicate His throne by having the Church abandon the truths of the Faith. There are also bolder attempts to overturn Christ's kingship through judicial arrogance. Today, you can read their opinions in the newspapers as they say: "We have no king but Caesar." It is a repetition of the moral arrogance that Pope Pius XI addressed when governments of his time attacked the sanctity of life through eugenics and social engineering.

Then as now, marriage was in the crosshairs, for if Caesar is to rule reality, he must be allowed to subvert natural law. This includes redefining marriage, the very core of civilization, an indissoluble bond between a man and a woman. It is significant that Pope Alexander III, who canonized St. Thomas Becket, that defender of Christ the King against an earthly ruler, also issued some four hundred decretals (papal edicts on doctrine or Church law) on the sanctity of marriage. Later attempts of the secretly married Protestant archbishop Cranmer to permit a system of divorce were not sanctioned for three centuries in English civil law. Even then, Lord Russell of Killowen lamented, "What was once a holy estate enduring for the joint lives of the spouses is steadily assuming the characteristics of a contract for a tenancy at will."

Cultural sanity can only return with obedience to the Kingship of Christ, and no congress, or supreme court, or synod can contradict him without contradicting its own integrity. In 1970, Blessed Pope Paul VI changed the feast of Christ the King to the climactic Sunday of the liturgical year, to declare to all the world that our Divine Sovereign "was and is and is to come." On that solemnity in 1997, St. John Paul II said:

> His was a shameful death, but it represents a confirmation of the Gospel proclamation of the kingdom of God. In the eyes of his enemies, that death should have been proof that all he had said and done was false: "He is the King of Israel; let him come down now from the cross, and we will believe in him" (Mt 27:42). He did not come down from the cross but, like the Good Shepherd, he gave his life for his sheep (cf. Jn 10:11). The confirmation of his royal power, however, came a little later when on the third day he rose from the dead, revealing himself as "the first-born of the dead" (Rv 1:5).

November 23, 2014

Shall God Be Driven From the Public Square?

The Statuary Hall in the Capitol in Washington has fifty statues, each representing a hero of each of the fifty states. Three of them are of Catholic priests: Father Eusebio Kino of Arizona, Blessed Junipero Serra of California, and Blessed Damien de Veuster of Hawaii.

These priestly presences may irritate the secularists who are trying to renovate our public buildings into temples of self-exaltation. The Ten Commandments are engraved on the Supreme Court building—where guides now refer to them as "Ten Amendments."[44] There are efforts to remove references to God from the burial rites in Arlington National Cemetery.

A visitors' center in the Capitol finally is being completed at a mind-boggling cost of $600 million of your tax money. Typical of government projects, its completion is several years late and hundreds of millions of dollars over budget. While its marble corridors will feature displays of Earth Day celebrations and AIDS rallies along with information about industry, it will ignore the Christian roots and heritage of our country. The original plans left out the national motto "In God We Trust," and the arrival of Christian missionaries was mentioned in passing as an "invasion." To date, 108 members of Congress have signed a petition against this disservice to history.

[44] Bob Unruh, "Ten Commandments Stunner: Feds Lying at Supreme Court," WND.com, November 14, 2006, http://www.wnd.com/.

It would be easy to exploit this out of demagoguery, and some politicians do indeed like to pose righteously protesting against "the removal of God" from our culture. That kind of rhetoric itself betrays some insecurity about God's ability to be God. God cannot be removed from anything because He is eternal and omnipresent. Attempts to marginalize God only marginalize those who try. The Catholic should understand this better than anyone, for the Holy Church outlives all nations and cultures. In the practical order, however, many nominal Catholics do not realize how they have been invaded by banal agnosticism and degraded by cultural mediocrity. Once in preparing a wedding, a bride from another part of the country wanted excerpts from Ernest Hemingway and Kahlil Gibran read as scripture in the sacrament of holy matrimony. Her reaction to my refusal was the indignation of an indulged youth who had never been denied access to a parallel universe of sentimental delights. It has been observed that even many self-styled Christians seek no Savior for they do not know that there is anything to be saved from.

A presidential proclamation of Thanksgiving Day enshrines a civic obligation to the Divine Creator, but for some it is a vestigial tribute to custom, encroached by football and parades. No president is a pontiff, and civic prayers are only commentary on the Eucharistic duty of the stewards of God's creation. So the feast of Christ the King, which we celebrate today, puts all civic intuitions of God into perspective, and reminds us that Jesus was crowned with thorns by self-satisfied people who hymned their way to destruction by shouting, "We have no king but Caesar" (John 19:15).

November 23, 2008

Evil to Resist; Holiness to Attain

Our former church was begun in 1857 and rebuilt after a fire in 1892. When I kneel before the high altar, which was moved to its present location in 1907 to make room for the Pennsylvania Station, I think of how the Holy Sacrifice of the Mass has been offered there through the Civil War with its draft riots and lynchings, and two World Wars, as well as Korea and Vietnam, with their victory parades and funerals for the young men killed in them. Workers and firemen who worshipped at this altar were killed at the World Trade Center. Every altar in the world is a focus of the human drama, and while Christ died once and rose in victory, never to die again, His death transcends time in His merciful union with all human suffering. This is why Pascal said paradoxically in his *Pensées* that the Risen Christ "is in agony on the Mount of Olives until the end of the world."

When the haters of remnant Christian civilization struck Paris last Friday the thirteenth, many kept saying that it was "unreal" and "inexplicable." But the blood was real, and the cruelty was totally explicable by the history of false religion and its embrace of evil. Fittingly, when the attack began in that concert hall, the band was playing a cacophonous piece, barely distinguishable from gunfire, called "Kiss the Devil." Only those afflicted with the illusion of secular progressivism as a substitute for the gospel seemed bewildered. Evil is real and explicable by the Fall of Man. Through the battles that have been fought and endured as Mass was being said on our altar, those who knelt here have promised to renounce Satan, and all his evil works, and all his empty promises.

It is different now that a whole generation has been taught to think that there is no evil to resist, and no holiness to attain. The highest ambition of our new, therapeutic culture is no loftier than the desire to "feel good" about oneself. We were solaced by politicians telling us that ISIS has been "contained" and is less dangerous than climate change. While Christians in the Middle East were being slaughtered in what the Pope himself called genocide—although our own State Department refused to call it that—coddled and foul-mouthed students on our college campuses were indulging psychodramatic claims of hurt feelings and low self-esteem. They are not the stuff of which civilization's heroes are made, and when the barbarians flood the gates, their teddy bears and balloons will be of little use.

Christ is the King of the Universe because "he is before all things and in him all things hold together" (Col. 1:17). To deny that is to be left in a moral whirlwind, thinking that evil is unreal and the actions of evil people have no explanation.

November 22, 2015

THE THRONE OF GRACE

Thanksgiving Day affords countless causes for thanks, not the least of which is that our nation got off to a good start with so many honest people trying to establish a society respectful of God and His blessings. George Washington proclaimed the first Thanksgiving Day in 1789. He had not planned on being president, though he knew that many wanted him. In 1783, after resigning his command of the army at a farewell in Annapolis, he mounted his horse and rode back to Mount Vernon. When the American-born painter Benjamin West told King George III that Washington had given up his power, the general's old foe said, "If he does that, he will be the greatest man in the world."

Earthly governance is part of the natural order for the establishment of the "tranquility of order," as St. Augustine taught. While bad rulers have been countless, there have also been saints who ruled with crown and scepter: Canute of the Danes, Charles of Flanders, David of Scotland, Edmund of East Anglia, Edward of England, Stephen of Hungary, Wenceslaus of Bohemia, Eric of Sweden, Louis of France, Ludwig of Thuringia, and most recently, Karl of Austria, to name but a few.

But as "uneasy lies the head that wears the crown," so too can the king lay heavy burdens on the people. The prophet Samuel warned the Jews against taking on a king, saying he would "take your sons and appoint them to his chariots.... He will take the tenth of your grain.... He will take the tenth of your flocks, and you shall be his slaves" (1 Sam. 8:10–17).

The excesses of bad rulers have been lurid in our time. Probably the worst right now is the communist imperium of North Korea, where the ruling Kim family has made itself a cult, punishing anyone who worships God instead of its hereditary leader. In that bizarre society, all international communications are banned, and anyone possessing a Bible is subject to execution. In the latest of many atrocities, on November 3, eighty Christians and other dissidents were shot before a crowd of ten thousand, including children forced to watch. Then their families were sent to almost certain death in prison camps.

The Holy Church appoints the last Sunday of the liturgical year as the feast of Christ the King, dedicating all human order to His rule. A venerable prayer begins: "O Lord our heavenly Father, the high and mighty Ruler of the universe, who dost from thy throne behold all the dwellers upon earth ..."

God's throne is the power of grace that holds all physical creatures in an ordered unity and inspires moral life toward eternal happiness. Without Him nothing holds together, and chaos reigns because, as one liturgical preface says, "Before him, all earthly rule is a shadow and a passing breath."

November 24, 2013

Sophia Institute

Sophia Institute is a nonprofit institution that seeks to nurture the spiritual, moral, and cultural life of souls and to spread the Gospel of Christ in conformity with the authentic teachings of the Roman Catholic Church.

Sophia Institute Press fulfills this mission by offering translations, reprints, and new publications that afford readers a rich source of the enduring wisdom of mankind.

Sophia Institute also operates two popular online Catholic resources: CrisisMagazine.com and CatholicExchange.com.

Crisis Magazine provides insightful cultural analysis that arms readers with the arguments necessary for navigating the ideological and theological minefields of the day. *Catholic Exchange* provides world news from a Catholic perspective as well as daily devotionals and articles that will help you to grow in holiness and live a life consistent with the teachings of the Church.

In 2013, Sophia Institute launched Sophia Institute for Teachers to renew and rebuild Catholic culture through service to Catholic education. With the goal of nurturing the spiritual, moral, and cultural life of souls, and an abiding respect for the role and work of teachers, we strive to provide materials and programs that are at once enlightening to the mind and ennobling to the heart; faithful and complete, as well as useful and practical.

Sophia Institute gratefully recognizes the Solidarity Association for preserving and encouraging the growth of our apostolate over the course of many years. Without their generous and timely support, this book would not be in your hands.

www.SophiaInstitute.com
www.CatholicExchange.com
www.CrisisMagazine.com
www.SophiaInstituteforTeachers.org